Stirring Up The African American Spirit

Ida Greene, Ph.D.

Stirring Up The African American Spirit

Ida Greene, Ph.D.

Stirring Up the African American Spirit, Copyright © April 3, 2007, by P. S. I. Publishers, 2910 Baily Ave. San Diego, CA 92105. All rights reserved. No part of this publication may be reproduced, distributed, transmitted, transcribed, stored in a retrieval system, or translated into any language without the express prior agreement and written permission of the publisher.

ISBN 1-881165-19-1
Library of Congress Card Catalog Number:

ATTENTION COLLEGES AND UNIVERSITIES, CORPORATIONS, AND PROFESSIONAL ORGANIZATIONS: Quantity discounts are available on bulk purchases of this book for educational training purposes, fund raising, or gift giving.
For information contact: **P. S. I. Publishers, 2910 Baily Ave. San Diego, CA 92105 (619) 262-9951.**

Acknowledgements

I am grateful that I was born an African American female in Pensacola, Florida. I am grateful to be a product of the segregated South. It taught me how to define and affirm my self worth and self esteem. Learning how to develop a positive self-image when southern whites in the fifty's and sixty's treated me as "inferior" and as a "no body." I had to develop a strong sense of "self" to counter the dominant societal beliefs that I was a "nobody." I decided to become a "somebody" and chose the path of education to accomplish my goal. These experiences helped me to develop a passion for self esteem which was destroyed in me (when I lived in the segregated South.)

I am grateful that my mom who had a third grade education wanted me to do better than her and prodded me daily to get an education. I am grateful for my father who believed in me, who always saw the possibilities in me, and encouraged me to achieve. My father always saw me as a leader and number one. I achieved and accomplished many things because it gave my father "pride" and satisfaction. I became the first in my family to graduate from High School. The first in my family to become a Registered Nurse. I was the first in my family to achieve a bachelor's degree, the first to achieve a Masters degree, and also the first in my family to achieve a Ph.D. Today I have a passion for education, learning, achieving, and improving the self esteem of children.

Introduction

To *Stir Up the African American Spirit*, these are the issues I will address: dating, sexuality, sensuality, racism, integration, interracial dating/marriage, role of the family, the extended family, what it means to grow up as part of a village and the sadness I feel over its demise. I include anything I feel will help us to remember who we are and why God created us as a race of people. We were created to shake the conscious of humanity. Now we need someone (myself) to awaken us to our true purpose and continue to strive for greatness.

You may see the words Afro-American interchanged with African American, or Black. The word Black is generic. It may be used by persons who are mulatto or of African descent but mixed with another race. Afro-American and African American, identifies one's connection to the continent Africa. These titles all depict philosophical positions, or points of reference used to encapsulate the pent up feelings of a people struggling to define themselves, and to become a free self-governing people who are in control of their own destiny.

The African American did not come to this country as a free person. They were captured as a hunted animal, placed on a slave ship, tied, and restrained with rope around their wrists, ankles, bodies, and made to lay side by side as if in a sardine can for the journey from Africa to the Americas. They landed in Virginia and were sold to merchants in the south who needed hired hands to till their crops and pick cotton. Cotton was the number one commodity in the
United States at that time. After they arrived on the shores of America they were sold as property to the highest bidder.

Looking back at the inception of African Americans upon the soil of the Americas, it becomes clear that they were treated in a subservient manner. African Americans were treated in an inhumane manner, which was accepted by society then. African Americans were taken in jest and viewed as childlike, comical, and stupid among whites. They lived in fear twenty four hours a day, that if they displeased their slave master they could be sold against their will to the highest bidder. African Americans had no rights. They were not protected under the laws of the state or country.

Our society continues to use color of skin as a measure of one's acceptance. The ideal worthwhile person is blond, blue eyed, may be male or female; the further removed one is from this standard determines his/her not being acceptable. Everything negative or bad in nature is dark or evil; therefore anyone with a less than white complexion will be scorned, rejected, or treated as less than. There is a belief by some Europeans that Africans, and African Americans, evolved from the ape/monkey, and are therefore wild, unruly, uncultured and animal in nature, with an uncontrolled sex drive. Africans were considered ignorant, stupid, child like, and with a brain smaller in weight and mass than that of whites. And their undeveloped brain affected their ability to understand complex information. Also African Americans are the only ethnic racial group in America who came to this country as indentured slaves and were not free people. In this role they were unable to make any decision for themselves or for their family, until they obtained their freedom.

I propose that African American/Blacks are unable to resolve the color dilemma by themselves, because they were not the creators of the stereotyped, prejudicial beliefs held about them. They did not establish institutionalized racism; likewise, they are not the perpetrators of mass media dissemination about the evils of being Black. Therefore they are powerless to change a system that victimizes them because of their skin color. Due to years of conditioning, African Americans need the support, and aid of all conscious, loving people of the human race to change their deeply, ingrained negative self-perception. With improved self-esteem, we begin to act empowered. The more we act empowered, the more we become who we were destined to be; a race of people equal to all people.

The key is an educated enlightened society who sees them as capable, competent, worthwhile people who are valuable and needed by society.

The book *Stirring Up The African American Spirit* touches on such issues as: AIDS, the Black Family, parenting, adoption, relationships, and homosexuality, down low's, business ownership, verbal/emotional abuse, domestic violence and religion.

Table of Contents

Acknowledgements ii

Introduction iii

Chapter 1 1
The Past Revisited

Chapter 2 18
Relationships, the Door to Everything

Chapter 3 37
In Search of the Black Family

Chapter 4 57
You and Your Relationship with Money

Chapter 5 80
Business Ownership, Key to Getting What You Want

Chapter 6 91
The Sex Revolution

Chapter 7 96
AIDS, What You Don't Know Can Kill You

Chapter 8 99
The Sellout of Jesus and the Black Church

Chapter 9 104
Domestic Violence, Emotional Abuse, It's Affect on the Family

Index 125

Bibliography 126

Testimonials 127

Chapter 1

THE PAST REVISITED

The American culture has many generalized erroneous perceptions of the African American. These perceptions are negative, limited, restrictive, fear laden, and stereotypical. The modern day African-American is a product of the African culture on the continent of Africa and a complex mixture of the confederate south. Most of the slaves were separated from their families and sold individually rather than as a family. They were established in the homes of a slave master. Many had kind slave masters, but most experienced abuse. All slaves were not respected; thought to be stupid and without intelligence. They came from different tribes and spoke the language of their tribe. They did not know how to speak, or read English. Most of them were forbidden to learn to read. Many caring children sneaked and taught slave children how to read. Some Africans, like Phyllis Wheatley learned to read on their own. This gave them a feeling of competence, self-respect, and added to their positive self-image and self-esteem.

The African settlers to America were uprooted from their families on both shores of Africa, and after they arrived in the United States.

They were thought to be unintelligent, child-like, easy to scare, wild, and like untamed animals. They were placed in chains like an animal, and sold on an auction block. This was degrading and dehumanizing. It accomplished the intended objective which was to instill fear, inferiority, and a mind set of servitude and enslavement. In addition, whites were considered the elite, and slaves were thought of as monetary property. They were valued for their brute strength and ability to work long hours in the sun. Slaves did not have the right to disagree with a request or demand made upon them; neither could they refuse the demand of anyone who was white. Even if the person was a child. Angela Y. Davis, in Women, Race and Class wrote, "Females, slave women were inherently vulnerable to all forms of sexual coercion. The most violent punishments of men consisted of flogging, (beatings) and mutilations. Most women were flogged, mutilated, and raped. Rape was a camouflaged expression of the slave holder's economic mastery, and the over-seer's control of Black women as workers."

In 1860, there were 488,070 free African-Americans and 4 million enslaved Africans in America. Most of them could not read or write, and had to learn any way they could. They used the Bible or relied on abolitionist-people who were against slavery-and young white children. Many stole books from the private libraries of their masters, or whites who employed them. And they sought out other African-Americans who could read and write.

According to Carter G. Woodson, "The Negro in Our History," In the 1700's Harry and Andrew, last name unknown started a school for slaves in Goose Creek Parish in South Carolina; they became the first African-Americans employed as teachers. During the early years of America's history, skin color was not important as it has become. As the country grew, rich white land owners decided to institute a more profitable employment system called slavery. Africans were forced to become slaves. The white men, who established the system, declared Africans as inferior and sub-human and skin color became the most important human characteristic in America. Color of skin determined who received respect, who was important, and who was treated as a person. Ones self-worth was based on skin color. Slaves were forbidden to learn to read or write. Therefore the self-esteem and self-image of the African-American is rooted in shame about one's skin color, and self-doubt about one's intelligence or ability to think.

African Americans have always been valued for what they did, not for who they were. So one's ability to make a worthwhile contribution to humanity has always been associated with who one was, and how one performed. African American women, men and children were treated like a child regardless of their age. And all whites were considered to be their masters. African Americans of all ages called white children "mister" and "miss"... This practice added to the destruction of their sense of self-worth, self-appreciation, and self-respect. It is self-degrading for an adult Black man to say "yes sir" and "no ma'am" to a child, the same age as his child; who he expects to respect him. To act in this manner put the man on the same level as his child, and reinforces the notion that he is half a man. A man-child is not a real man because he has no control over his life, his family's welfare, or the circumstances that confront them. As a child I saw my father placed in this situation. It made him very strict, and demanding of respect from the five of us, and my mom.

In the past and still today, the Black man still thirst for self-respect, and has a shattered, distorted, self-concept and self-image. Any attempts to develop self-respect or self-pride were further eroded through institutionalized separatism of the races. This separation between Blacks and Whites existed at all public establishments even public water fountains.

In Pensacola, Florida where I grew up, Blacks were not allowed to eat at the lunch counter with whites. We were not permitted to drink from the same water fountains as whites. The water fountains were separated and labeled colored and whites only. We attended separate schools, lived in separate neighborhoods, and we had to sit in the back seats of all public transportation. The signs read "white" and "colored." Neither could I try on shoes in a shoe store. It was believed that skin would contaminate the shoe. This was a normal practice in Pensacola, Florida until 1969.

A young black British journalist wrote, "I'm foreign, so I do not have the legitimate traumatic baggage that African Americans have with (racism) even though I can see it all going on. I've got different traumas… I did get a whiff- which I knew intellectually, but it rarely came to the fore front like this- the fact that white people in the South really don't give a shit if I'm British or not. In 1970, I stopped to ask for directions from three old white people and they threatened to shoot me, and one of them went to get his gun. That's when I left. I thought "they're not going to shoot me." Why would they do that? But then I thought "Well maybe they will; this was an eye opening experience for me."

Because of all the emotional abuse I endured in the South, I still find myself struggling at time with low self-esteem, feelings of low self-worth, and a distorted self-image that tells me I am inferior to whites.
One can not be chained in shackles all their lives, abruptly have the physical and emotional shackles removed, then, told they are free human beings. Adults, no longer "children," and begin thinking and behaving as independent free adults.

It is easy to remove a physical shackle or chain. However, it may take centuries to unchain a shackled mind.

The mind and psyche of all African Americans, whether they lived in the liberal north or in the Klu, Klux clan, confederate south, continue to be shackled, and chained due to years of conditioning.

All African Americans living in the south lived in fear of over stepping their boundaries, of getting out of their place, and being reminded through a stare, a cold shoulder treatment, or through emotional isolation, that they were still sub-human and undeserving of respect as a human being.

It is very challenging to remove the mental, or emotional shackles of an enslaved mind that send out continual messages: "beat up on me," "I am not o.k., but you are o.k.," "I am worthless," "I need someone other than myself to validate me," "I am not sure if I am as smart as whites, or other races of people," "I can't think to figure things out for myself, I need to use the brains of someone other than myself," "My brains are no good, and will therefore not work for me," "I am not as valuable as whites," "I am stupid," "I am inferior," "My mind won't work for me, you do not like my looks, and neither do I," "My skin color is dark, my lips are thick, my nose is wide and large, I do not look like those I see on television or on the magazine covers and I am different," "I wish my skin color was lighter, I wish I were a lighter skin color" "There is something abnormal about my skin coloration." When we were children, innocently playing, we stated this phrase to each other on a daily basis, "If you are brown stick around, if you are black, step back, if you are white, you are alright." All of these are self-denial and self-rejection phrases.

I remember as a teenager, buying a container of skin bleaching cream to lighten my skin. Even though I was a pretty shade of brown, I did not see nor acknowledge this to myself, until I was told this by a white friend, later in San Diego California in the 80's.

In Pensacola Florida, I could not be seen playing with my white friend as a child. It was acceptable with her mother for us to be friends; however she asked that we not be seen together in public because she feared what might happen to her daughter. I was thought to be inferior to a fourteen year old white girl. Can you imagine the emotional scarring; an innocent action like this produces? I have been working on my self-esteem ever since I left Pensacola Florida, healing one layer at a time.

Due to the conditioning factor of spaced repetition, our mind remembers and retains what it hears. Our minds retain all information, whether it is to our benefit or not. You only need to reject yourself once, to set in motion self-denial, self-rejection pattern. Blacks are ridiculed, and humiliated by whites and other races of people. And we in turn ridicule, humiliate, and reject ourselves and other Blacks. This is a behavior we need to be mindful to avoid.

Some African Americans bought their freedom from their slave master. An industrious and persevering individual was Alonzo Herndon, who lived from 1858-1927, and turned $11.00 from savings into a fortune to become America's first African-American millionaire. He started as a barber with only white clients. He wrote, "I started out alone with a five-chair shop. By unceasing watchfulness of my business and being tactful, I showed manly conduct toward my Southern patrons with whom I am happy to say, I have always had the most pleasant esteem and have every reason to believe my business is held. I have grown from five barber chairs to twenty-five, employing nearly forty men," When the state passed a law in 1905 requiring insurance companies to deposit $5,000 with the state treasurer, Mr. Herndon purchased nine small burial associations. He organized them into the Atlanta Mutual Insurance Association. That association later became the Atlanta Life Insurance Company, now the second largest African-American Life Insurance Company in the nation. Atlanta Life provided insurance and mortgages to low income Blacks who were unable to obtain these services elsewhere. The company also provided professional, managerial and clerical jobs to African-Americans. Mr. Herndon was worth $1.1 million at the time of his death in 1927.

Children as well as adults learn from society about their self-worth, self-image, and self-importance. If references have been made, and put in print, that they have the brain of an ape, that they are the offspring of a gorilla, that their brain mass is smaller than that of whites, if everything said about them in books is negative or degrading, they will eventually believe it. Also if a person is told or made to believe a given statement is factual, even though it may be a conjecture with limited evidential fact, it will be accepted as true by the mind. This is especially true if the information is stated over a medium such as television.

Our self-esteem is a blue print of who we are, how we have been treated, respected, appreciated, and identified by those around us, and our external family. The self-image is a by product of the self-esteem. It reflects how we picture ourselves; how we honor, respect, and value ourselves. It paints a mental picture from our inner belief of who we think we can be, or what we believe we can do in life. These words by a noted speaker address self-worth.

A well-known speaker started off his seminar by holding up a $20.00 bill. In the room of 200 people, he asked, "Who would like this $20 bill?" Hands started going up. He said, "I am going to give this $20 to one of you but first, let me do this. He proceeded to crumple up the $20 dollar bill. He then asked, "Who still wants it?" Still the hands were up in the air. Well, he replied, "What if I do this?" And he dropped it on the ground and started to grind it into the floor with his shoe. He picked it up, now crumpled and dirty. "Now, who still wants it?" Still the hands went into the air. My friends, we have all learned a very valuable lesson. No matter what I did to the money, you still wanted it because it did not decrease in value. It was still worth $20.

Many times in our lives, we are dropped, crumpled, and ground into the dirt by the decisions we make and the circumstances that come our way. We feel as though we are worthless. But no matter what has happened or what will happen, you will never lose your value. Dirty or clean, crumpled or finely creased, you are still priceless to those who LOVE you. The worth of our lives comes not in what we do or who we know, but by WHO WE ARE. You are special; always remember this.

THE INVITATION

It doesn't interest me what you do for a living
I want to know what you ache for, and if you dare to dream
of meeting your heart's longing. It doesn't interest me how
old you are.
I want to know if you will risk looking like a fool for love,
for your dreams, for the adventure of being alive.

It doesn't interest me what planets are squaring your moon,
I want to know if you have touched the center of your own
sorrow, if you have been opened by life's betrayals or have
become shriveled and closed from fear of further pain.

I want to know if you can sit with pain, mine or your own, without moving to hide or fake it or fix it.
I want to know if you can be with joy, mine or your own; if you can dance with wildness and let ecstasy fill you to the tips of your fingers and toes without cautioning us to be careful, be realistic, or to remember the limitations of being human.

It doesn't interest me if the story you're telling me is true. I want to know if you can disappoint another to be true to yourself,
If you can bear the accusation of betrayal and not betray your own Soul.
I want to know if you can see beauty, even if it's not pretty every day, And if you can source your life from God's presence.
I want to know if you can live with failure, yours and mine, and still stand on the edge of a lake and shout to the silver of the full moon, "YES!"
It doesn't interest me to know where you live or how much money you have.

I want to know if you can get up after a night of grief and despair, wary and Bruised to the bone, and do what needs to be done for the children.
It doesn't interest me who you are, how you came to be here. I want to know if you Will stand in the center of the fire with me and not shrink back.
It doesn't interest me where or what or with whom you have studied.
I want to know what sustains you from the inside when all else falls away.
I want to know if you can be alone with yourself,
And if you truly like the company you keep in the empty moments.

    Oriah Mountain Dreamer, Indian Elder, May 1994

Christmas Watch Night Services,
A New Meaning of "Watch Night Services"

Many of you who live or grew up in Black communities in the United States have probably heard of "Watch Night Services," the gathering of the faithful in church on New Year's Eve. The service usually begins anywhere from 7 p.m. to 10 p.m. and ends at midnight with the entrance of the New Year. Some folks come to church first, before going out to celebrate. For others, church is the only New Year's Eve event. Like many others, I always assumed that Watch Night was a fairly standard Christian religious service, made a bit more Afro centric because that's what happens when elements of Christianity become linked with the Black Church. Still, it seemed that predominately White Christian churches did not include Watch Night services on their calendars, but focused instead on Christmas Eve programs. In fact, there were instances where clergy in mainline denominations wondered aloud about the propriety of linking religious services with a secular holiday like New Year's Eve.

However, there is a reason for the importance of New Year's Eve services in African American congregations. The Watch Night Services in Black communities that we celebrate today can be traced back to gatherings on December 31, 1862, also known as "Freedom's Eve." On that night, Blacks came together in churches and private homes all across the nation, anxiously awaiting news that the Emancipation Proclamation actually had become law. Then, at the stroke of midnight, on January 1, 1863, all slaves in the Confederate States were declared legally free. When the news was received, there were prayers, shouts and songs of joy as people fell to their knees and thanked God. Since then Black people have gathered in churches annually on New Year's Eve, praising God for bringing them safely through another year. It's been 141 plus years since that first Freedom's Eve and many of us were never taught the African American history of Watch Night, but tradition still brings us together at this time every year to celebrate "how we got over. Sometimes we lose sight of the things that gave us passion in the past.

The Great Things of Life

Oscar Wilde addresses the passions our fore fathers had that many of us today are struggling to find.
The great things of life are not what they seem to be.
And for that reason, strange as it may sound to you,
are often very difficult to interpret.
Great passions are for the great of soul,
And great events can only be seen by those who
are on a level with them.
We think we can have our visions for nothing.
We cannot. Even the finest and most self-sacrificing have to be paid for. Strangely enough, that is what make them fine." Oscar Wilde

Playing Small

Our deepest fear is not that we are inadequate.
Our deepest fear is that we are powerful beyond measure.
It is our Light, not our Darkness, that most frightens us.
We ask ourselves, who am I to be brilliant, gorgeous, talented, and fabulous?
Actually, who are you NOT to be? You are a child of God.
Your playing small does not serve the World.
There is nothing enlightened about shrinking
so that other people won't feel insecure around you.
We were born to make manifest the glory of God that is within us.

*It is not just in some of us; it is in everyone.
As we let our own Light shine, we unconsciously
give other people permission to do the same.
as we are liberated from our own fear, our presence
automatically liberates others.*
              Marianne Williamson

It is always best for our self-esteem and self-confidence to not quit or give up on ourselves. In life we will always be tested. We gain emotional muscles when we do not fold, give up or quit. God never gives us more than we can handle. God will give us the strength to handle anything we feel is impossible to do.

Every time we overcome an obstacle, our character and resolve becomes stronger and we can endure more. The words that run through my head whenever I am tempted to quit anything is the short commencement speech Winston Churchill gave to a graduation class. He said "Never Give Up, Never Give Up, Never, Ever, Ever Give Up" then he sat down in his seat. I have never given up or said no to anything in my life.

I grew up in tough times, during the 50's, that have toughened my resolve. When I grew up in the south, quitting was not an option. Neither was suicide, so we had to rely on our faith to see us through every problem. We just found a way to solve every problem. We were always told that Jesus said "If you take one step I will take two", we took that one step, whatever it was, and God did make a way out of no way. My mother always said "God will make a way out of no way" and I have found that to be true. We get strong from going through a trial not by running away; Giving up and telling ourselves it won't work or that we are incapable. Whatever you decide, it's your choice and will work for or against you.

My Long Lost Brother
from the euro by Steven Ivory

Saturday afternoon at the counter of a crowded café, a fifty something stranger in sweats and a worn Nike T-shirt who says he is a banker is telling me a story about approving a business loan to a customer at his branch. He is particularly proud to green light the transaction, he says, because he believes the customer's idea is a brilliant one. I don't ask what the idea is; I am too entranced with his passing description of the customer, whom he refers to as a "Brother."

A Brother. A term so indigenous to modern America that a nerdy white banker cordially tosses it about without the slightest trace of patronization though, in retrospect, I guess it was patronization, since he probably would not have used the term to describe that black customer to a white person); a phrase so congenital that whole generations don't know that, officially, from days gone by, it is Soul Brother and Soul Sister.

Today, the word "soul" may evoke images of afros, African dashikis and fists raised in a symbol of black power, but when Soul Brother was embraced by mid 1960s colored folk, it was a unifying phrase of endearment and reprieve from the demeaning connotation of the word Negro. Presumably, a Soul Brother or Sister was someone with a discerning sense of cultural pride and self love. Of course, soul itself is even deeper: It is the essence, the sum and substance of a thing. The soul is the beginning, the foundation and the foremost. Therefore, the soul of a man is who he is, what he is about and what he is worth. A people began to call themselves brothers and sisters at a time when they desperately needed to rescue themselves from doubt and lack of direction. But blacks don't use the "Soul" word much anymore. What was once a bold, prideful concept now seems antiquated? When the word is used today, there seems a concerted effort to somehow refurbish or neuter it. Thus, "Soul Food" has evolved into "Southern American Cuisine" or some other moniker, streamlined and otherwise innocuous.

    Likewise, tragically, some music executive, attempting to put a new spin on a classic genre, is no doubt the genius who championed the term "Neo Soul"--as if, on a good day D'Angelo, Maxwell, Eryka Badu and Jill Scott recall anything but the likes of soul greats Curtis Mayfield, Marvin Gaye, Miles Davis, Betty Davis, a Stevie Wonder-produced Syreeta or Chaka Khan. NEO-soul?

    This is not about music or collard greens, though. Music and all other forms of expression, creative and impassioned, is merely a product of the soul. Soul is not the Train, platform shoes and afro puffs; those are but styles and trends. Soul is the essence, a valiant approach to living not defined by or relegated to color or race.

    Nevertheless, no matter how hip he appeared, I would never tell that white banker of my melancholy that a generation of brothers and sisters increasingly appears disconnected from its collective soul.

    Whatever became of my brother's personal pride? Not the arrogant, self-serving sense of entitlement and respect only for what he can purchase, but the inspired self love that he exhibited back when he had but himself and a dream? Why is my sister not embarrassed at the way she carries her person? And how has she allowed herself to buy into the hellish misogyny that defines her merely as an object to be used and taken advantage of?

When I think of the young men who slay one another in the name of some twisted ritual of urban territory that neither of them owns, it makes me sad.   When I glimpse the buffoonery of sinister, trifling video images so vividly crafted for the entire world to interpret, it makes me angry. And when he walks past me on the street without issuing so much as a nod and doesn't acknowledge my greeting to him, it causes me to ponder in silent wonder: What, in God's name has become of you soul, Brother?

Random Quotes

"One single grateful thought raised to Heaven is the most perfect prayer."
Author unknown

"True prayer is not only expressed by your tongue but by your thoughts and actions as well. Synchronize all three and your prayers will be answered."
Author unknown

Let Nothing Disturb Your Peace of Mind
"Be so strong that nothing can disturb your peace of mind. Talk health, happiness, and prosperity to every person you meet. Make all your friends feel there is something special in them.
Look at the sunny side of everything.
Think only of the best, work only for the best, and expect only the best.
Be as enthusiastic about the success of others as you are about your own. Forget the mistakes of the past and press on to the greater achievements of the future.
Give everyone a smile. Spend so much time improving yourself that you
have no time left to criticize others.
Be too big for worry and too noble for anger."
Author Unknown

"It doesn't interest me what you do for a living
I want to know what you ache for, and
If you dare to dream of meeting your heart's longing
It doesn't interest me how old you are
I want to know if you will risk looking like a fool for love,
For your dream, for the adventure of being alive ... "
 The Invitation - Oriah Mountain Dreamer

Follow your heart and go with your gut.
This is the path to your Soul Purpose.
This is the way toward discovering and
Fulfilling your Destiny.
From the Heart to the Soul

Chapter 2

Relationships, The Door to Everything

According to Harold Sherman, the more you depend on forces outside yourself, the more you are dominated by them. Lately relationships between Black men and women seem to be on a collision course. I am not sure who or what is to blame, however I can point to some factors that has made and continues to make communicating and relating between Black men and women a challenge. Here are some of the factors: Integration, blending or melting of the races. All races of women have heard about the myth of the big black penis that stays hard 24 hours of the day, so they want to try the latest fad of having sex with a black man. I over heard two white girls talking about how big, long and hard it was, I knew one of them was referring to her sexual experience with a Black man. It does not matter whether the myth about the Black man's sexual organs is true or false; there are a lot of myths and fantasizing about his genitals. They seem to care less about his mind, his personality, ability to provide for them or give them love; they just want a penis that stays hard supposedly 24 hours of the day. They really want a mule or horse penis, not a human being. However the fantasy continues to be perpetuated by white men, white women and Black men to some extent.

The reasons Black men give for dating and having sex with women of other races are many. Some Black men have been heard to say they want variety, that the sisters are not giving up sex easily, and they have to work too hard to get sex from a Black woman. Yet I have heard some Black men say they want someone who will give them no lip (argument) and will do as they are told like the Mexican women. Yet another factor seem to be the availability of

Black men willing and wanting to date women of other races-forbidden fruit-(white, Mexican, Asian and Filipino). However some reasons given by Black men is that being involved with a woman of other races: They are easier to get along with, they (women) of other races take care of me financially, they have access to money, they like kinky sex, they let me do what I want, they don't hassle me, they make a big fuss over me, it makes me feel loved and it seem that they care.

These are some of the reasons they give for not being in relationship with Black women: They are too demanding. They are tight with their money. They like to argue, they are too controlling. I can't get sex when I want it. Black professional women don't want a poor brother with no money." I am sure you can add to the list. What do I feel is behind all of this? It is probably all of these issues plus some beliefs that I have not listed.

According to Jafree a soul mate is someone whom you experience a deep intimate connection and profound synchronicity with. You can often have the feeling that each moment truly feels "timeless" together, and upon your first meeting you may feel as if you have known each other for many years. You may also feel like you can share anything you are experiencing in your life without editing your words or holding back in any way. There is this simple presence together, and a closeness that allows you to relax with this person and be yourself.

The truth is there are many people on the planet that can fit into this description of being your soul mate. You don't have to yearn and search for years to locate that one and only one person (out of 6.5 billion) if you wish to experience a fulfilling love life. You can have a deeper profound loving connection with many people, and experience this satisfying soul connection with them every day.

So what is stopping you from manifesting your soul mate? Often the negative experiences from the past can block our heart from trusting love, and create an impenetrable wall of defense, blocking your soul mate from finding you. If your heart is still holding onto previous wounds or negative experiences from relationships in your past, you may feel that it's "too" dangerous to let love in, and is busy trying to protect itself from getting hurt again. The interesting thing is that your wall does not allow in any pain or feelings of being loved. The wall blocks both the positive and negative experiences, leaving you completely void of personal intimate relationships.

Even though you may not think you have a "wall" around your heart, you can always practice letting more love in. The melting and healing of even the smallest of walls is one of the greatest keys to manifesting your soul mate. If you have been with someone for many years and you still feel that they are not your soul mate, it is very possible that a mini-defense wall was put up, and is not allowing you to FEEL the deeper intimate soul connection you have with them. This happens more frequently than you think.

Many people who are together for years often find themselves feeling stuck, blocked or blame their partner for not being able to move deeper into the relationship. They may experience a variety of negative thoughts and feelings about their partner and themselves. They may find that the intimacy between them has become a game of shielding themselves. This again is caused by unhealed wounds from the past and can be changed through healing the heart and re-connecting your soul with their heart in your inner world. Always remember...your inner world manifests your outer world. When you are experiencing a deep loving intimate connection with your "inner mate", he or she will manifest into your outer world. When your heart is open and ready to receive the experience of being loved without fear of abandonment, rejection, or pain, your soul mate will surface and show up physically in your outer world.

    There are many things you can do to manifest an amazing relationship. Often the most empowering methods are also the most challenging. One vital aspect to manifesting an amazing relationship is keeping your focus on what you like about that person, instead of what you don't like. Whatever you put your attention on expands and grows, so why not look for what is sweet rather than sour? Anytime you find something negative in someone, there is some part of you desperately at work trying to change them, which is also secretly judging them for not being what they "should" be. The Universe is always exactly the way it should be in every moment; realize this and you've just become more enlightened.

    Something else that will increase your sense of inner peace within any relationship is to realize the world is your mirror. What this means is the relationships you create with others, are mirror reflections of what is inside you. Are you aware that the mirror is always reflecting, if you do not judge yourself for what you see outside yourself, you are guaranteed to have successful relationships? This poem says a lot about relationships.

Relationships Are at Risk

To laugh is to risk appearing the fool
To weep is to risk appearing sentimental.
To reach out to another is to risk involvement.
To expose feelings is to risk exposing our true self.
To place our ideas, our dreams, before the crowd
is to risk loss.
To love is to risk not being loved in return.
To live is to risk dying.
To hope is to risk despair.
To try is to risk failure.
But To Risk We Must, Because the Greatest Hazard in Life
is to Risk Nothing, For the Man or Woman Who Risks
Nothing, Does Nothing, Has Nothing, is Nothing
                    ANON

Do You Have Low or High Self-Esteem?
Some Signs Are:
1. Being overly sensitive
2. Defensiveness - Deep within you are afraid that you are wrong.
3. Self hate; Difficulty in loving others.
4. Compulsive habits such as over eating.
5. Shy- uncomfortable in social situations.
6. Afraid to risk- don't want to make a fool of yourself, so you don't try.
7. Do not have close friends.
8. Criticizes yourself and others.
9. Impatient with self "Have a lot of "I should"
10. Chronic physical condition. False separation from God; Your
11. God self and human self are one and the same.
12. Persistent money problems.

WHAT'S YOUR BEHAVIORAL STYLE?

Director	Socializer	Relator	Thinker
Dominance	Emotional	Steady	Perfection
Doer	Expressive	Stable	Compliant
Leader	Disorganized	Loyal	Competent
Ego Oriented	Inspirational	Listener	Problem Solver
Opinionated	Persuader	Likes Status Quo	Facts
Creative	Spontaneous	Patient	Rules
Direct	Playful	Warm	Cautious
Competitive	Enthusiastic	Friendly	Accurate
Aggressive	Interactive	Supportive	Detailed
Decisive	Trusting	Amicable	Analytical
Business Like	Optimistic	Predictable	High Standards
Driving	Charming	Complacent	Data
Demanding	Motivator	Sincere	Correct
Blunt	Fashionable	Team Player	Planner

Check only words that most represent your behavioral style

TREAT PEOPLE THE WAY THEY WANT TO BE TREATED

Communication is the Foundation of Successful Relationship, So Watch Your Mouth

1. Let go of defensive communication:
2. You don't need it. There are better ways to reinforce yourself. Nothing really gets defended or preserved by it.
3. Live by this formula: 2+2=10 times 1:
4. Your ears (listening) and your eyes (attending and focusing) are usually far more valuable when leading and trying to influence persuasively than your mouth, even though you are articulate.
5. Train your tongue to avoid cliques.
6. "I know how you feel, but, you just don't understand, well I'm not perfect, what is your problem anyway? Why did you do that?
7. Keep your cool under fire.

Utilize the test: one-year-from-now-will-it-matter?
Try the Earthquake safety slogan: "Duck, cover, and hold" you yourself are not (usually) the target.
Accept one of the facts of life -- that life is not fair.

Resolving to do good does not grant us full coverage in our relationship communications. <u>The more complex the interchange the more important is listening.</u>

We usually go hyper and talk more. It's hard to make a mistake or hurt someone's feelings when listening. *"I can't hear what you're telling me; until I am really sure you have understood what I feel and have heard what I am saying."*

"Improve Your Listening Skills" Exercise

Name_____

Hear the implicit I-statement in someone's message especially if the person is not speaking clearly, for you to understand. Evaluate the following statements:

What has been said to me	My active listening, or what that person might be feeling when he or she says that.
Get out of here!	I think he's mad- and getting madder by the minute. He doesn't want to deal with me at all right now. He wants to be alone.
If you loved me, you'd let me go	It sounds like she wants this really badly. It must feel to her like I don't love her when I tell her I don't want her to go.

21 THINGS AFRICAN AMERICANS NEED TO DO ACCORDING TO TAVIS SMILEY...

1. Register to vote, or shut up!
2. Take all that money out of those stocking caps, in cans, mattresses, and floorboards and invest money in something. For starters, invest in the food you eat and clothes you wear.
3. Learn another language. Ebonics does not count.

4. Stop using the "N" word, especially since Merriam-Webster has announced it isn't changing the definition.
5. Buy something each week from a black vendor.
6. Stop blaming white folks for 98% of your problems, while giving them 100% of your money.
7. Subscribe to Ebony, JET, Black Enterprise, Essence. Then subscribe to one of the three weeklies: Time, Newsweek, or US News and World Report. After we read about what's going on in our world, how about knowing what's going on in theirs? It is, after all, your world.
8. Stop walking past each other and not speaking.
9. Be on time for something, anything!
10. Get an annual check up; herbs do not cure everything!
11. In all thy ways acknowledge Him (GOD) and He shall direct thy path." prioritize this as # 1.
12. Stop being jealous of one another, learn to look past the material things and see the person for who they are.
13. Get involved in at least one charitable or voluntary community service.
14. Say a prayer for someone besides yourself.
15. Hug your child/spouse/parent today.
16. Love One Another.
17. Learn to Let Go and Let God.
18. Stop talking about it, and be about it.
19. Let GOD order your steps instead of the world.
20. P.U.S.H.! Pray Until Something Happens.
21. In all that you do, get understanding, (turn off the TV, and open a book).
22. Don't just read this, DO IT and encourage others to take nothing for granted.

Relationships, The Path to Fulfillment

Our relationships are the glue that keeps us connected to God, the universe and to people who inhabit the universe. We cannot live alone; we need the help of other people. However when we have been hurt, betrayed, abandoned, or rejected, we are less likely to reach out to others. My mother used to say, "A burnt child fears fire". I would like to add to that and say, a wounded and hurt ego fears rejection or a loss of acceptance. We tend to equate acceptance with approval, love and a belief that we are o.k. We assume and interpret non-acceptance and disapproval as a lack of caring or love.

I contend that if you have good relating skills, you can get or have anything you want. Relating to others is the core of everything we do. Since we cannot do everything ourselves, we have to rely on the help of others to help us accomplish our goals. To be successful or accomplish great wealth will require us to tap into the inner resources of others. What is your communication or relating IQ? Are you aware how you connect or communicate with others?

Problem Solving Techniques

All couples face conflict periodically. Even in the most ideal relationship, periods of discord are inevitable. One of the hallmarks of a successful relationship is the ability to resolve disputes in a way that is satisfying to both parties.

A relationship problem usually involves the desire for some kind of change on the part of at least one partner. Usually, one person has a complaint about some aspect of the other person's behavior. Examples are one person's desire that the other share more of the household chores, or a complaint that the other person talks too much.

Problem solving is a specialized activity, a structured interaction designed to resolve a particular dispute. It is not necessarily going to seem spontaneous, natural, or relaxing, especially at first. It is hard work, but it is worth it. The following are a set of guidelines for effective problem solving.

The Setting for Problem Solving

Problem solving should occur at a neutral and pre-arranged time, when both of you are calm and can give your attention to the problem. Don't try to resolve your dispute "at the scene of the crime." When we are emotionally aroused, as we are bound to be when a partner behaves undesirably, we are unlikely to problem solve in a rational manner.

Problem solving sessions should be relatively short, maybe thirty minutes for one problem. Never go beyond an hours, or try to solve more than two problems at a session. There should be an agenda, and each partner should take responsibility for bringing up issues. You may want to keep a notebook, recording the important elements of each session. At the top of the page, write the date, underneath, record the problem discussed and the agreement reached.

Problem Solving Attitude

The two keys to problem solving that will improve your relationship are ***collaboration*** and ***compromise.*** Typically, when distressed couples deal with conflict, the event takes the form of a power struggle. If the wife has gripe about the husband, he adopts a rigid posture and regards her gripe as a threat. If he agrees to change, it feels like he is losing face. He waits for his partner to change first. Meanwhile, the wife is doing the same thing. It is easy to see how couples reach stalemates with this view.

This rigid posture makes some sense; after all, in the short run a partner who "gives" is sacrificing something, especially if the change is not reciprocated. In the long run, the refusal to change is self-defeating for one's personal happiness, because as long as the relationship remains distressed and that person stays in it, he or she will be unhappy. So even if the complaint is your partner's all relationship problems are mutual problems

Our plea for collaboration does not mean that you must always agree to behave in a way that is satisfying to your partner. Some requests are unreasonable the plea is simply to maintain a collaborative spirit. A readiness to consider changing to make one's partner happier must be viewed in terms of its long-term benefits to the relationship, rather than simply in terms of its immediate cost to the person who is changing.

How to Define the Problem

Defining the problem is different from solving it. Problem definition means making a clear, specific statement of the problem, understood by both parties. No solutions are to be proposed until the problem is defined.

Guidelines for Defining the Problem

These guidelines mainly apply to the person who is bringing up the problem.

1. When stating a problem, begin with something positive whenever possible.

The purpose of this is to maintain your partner's collaborative spirit.

With Positive	*Without the Positive*
I appreciate the way you have been helping me around the house. Don't think I haven't noticed.	You don't help me clean up after dinner

No one likes to be criticized: we automatically feel attacked. .It is easier to accept criticism if you are being reminded that you're cared about. That doesn't mean that you should invent phony praise. Most couples don't need to "invent" expressions of appreciation. Actually, telling your partner what you like is a good thing to do frequently, and if you do it fairly often, and not just during problem solving session, your appreciation is more likely to be accepted at face value.

2. Use Good Expressive (Speaking) Communication Skills. Be specific. Describe the behavior that is bothering you. This will make it easier to make specific requests for a positive change.

Avoid making inferences about the other person's intentions: for example, "You were trying to humiliate me." Whether the other person was trying to humiliate you or not doesn't change the fact that you felt humiliated and would like your partner to behave differently in the future.

Express your feelings. Use I-messages and follow all the other rules for good communication that you have learned. Avoid generalizations: for example, "You never clean up the mess," or "You're always late." Avoid derogatory labels, such as "inconsiderate," "lazy," and "cold." Avoid name calling, too; for example "bitch," or "stupid." If you find it impossible to give up those words, re-examine your purpose in bringing up the problem. Chances are you were more concerned about expressing anger or getting back at your partner than with solving the problem. The same hold true for more sophisticated labels like "hysterical," "sadistic," or "introverted." The issue is not, "what personality traits does this person have" but, 'What is it about this person's behavior that I want to see changed?" **Be brief,** problem solving is oriented toward changing things in the future: Couples can spend an excessive amount of time talking about the problem. This increase the probability of an argument. Try to avoid overly detailed reviews of every example of the problem. A focus on the past causes may be interesting and relevant, but it can also be a way to avoid shifting the focus to the future. Similarly, avoid "why" questions. These can usually be restated as I-messages: for example, "why do you leave your socks on the floor?" really means "I don't like it when you leave your socks on the floor." **Admit to your role in the problem** right from the start. This is likely to increase your partner's willingness to collaborate rather than getting defensive. The next guidelines apply to both the complainer and the recipient of the complaint.

3. Discuss Only One Problem At a Time
Avoid cross-complaining and kitchen-sinking. When we are criticized, it is all too easy to bring other issues into the discussion. One of the reasons couples find problem solving so difficult is that they try to solve every problem in the relationship at once. That makes the task overwhelming. Both of you should take responsibility for staying on target. When you notice that the conversation has drifted off track, bring the discussion back to the original topic by saying, "We're supposed to be

discussing..." If the side issue is important enough to discuss, it deserves a problem solving session of its own.

4. Use Your Skills In Validating/Active Listening

It is extremely important to use these skills throughout your problem solving session. Summarize your partner's last remark before you respond. Check with your partner to make sure that the message you have heard was what he or she was trying to send. If there is a misunderstanding, it can be corrected immediately. In addition, making summary statements helps both of you see things from the other person's perspective. All too often we're preparing a rebuttal while the other person is talking instead of really listening. Paraphrasing or active listening forces you to slow down and listen to your partner's whole statement before you reply, and this is particularly important during problem solving.

5. Generating Solutions

Once you have stated the problem, shift your focus to possible solutions. The discussion should be future oriented and should answer the question, "What can we do to eliminate this problem and keep it from coming back?" At this point do not return to a restatement of the complaint.

6. Brainstorming

Brainstorming means both of you generating as many possible solutions to the problem as you can think of. Write down as you think of them. Use your imagination and even include some that may seem silly or absurd.

7. Remember Mutuality and Compromise

Both of you should be thinking about the problem in these terms:

A. What do I really want?
B. What am I willing to settle for?

Your answer to B should always be different from your answer to A. Too often people tend to see behaviors in all-or-none terms and to request sweeping changes: for example, he either helps with the kids or he doesn't. But your partner is more likely to agree to change in a small way rather than a sweeping way. Another strategy is to think, and to ask out loud, "How can I help you change?" For example, one couple was in conflict about who should put the children to bed at night. His complaint was that she always interfered when he tried to manage the children. So the way she could best help him to change was by remaining silent and totally out of the way while he was putting the kids to bed, even if he didn't do it just he way she would have done it.

8. How to Reach An Agreement
Now it is time to review all the possibilities. You might want to review them out loud, or make a chart.

Problem Solving Worksheet

Problems:	For/ Pros	Against/Cons

Possible solutions
Keep combining ideas and generating new ideas until an agreement is reached. Then put your agreement in writing. That way both of you will be able to refer back to it. Remember, keep your change agreements specific and describe behavior. For example:

Non-specific: Patty will not be as apprehensive about the future and will have more confidence in Don.

Specific: Patty will respond positively to Don when he starts to talk about his job. During these conversations, she will not make pessimistic remarks about the future of the company.

Sometimes the problem is not that a person is unwilling to comply with the request, but that when the time comes, he or she simply forgets. This is particularly likely with long-standing habits. In such cases the agreement should include some way of reminding the person what he or she agreed to. An example of an external cue would be a husband placing a little sign on the dashboard of his car which read "EFTS." This means "expressing his feelings to Sue" which was his own cue to do so.

Tell People What They Mean to You Today.

Summary of Steps for Effective Problem Solving

1. Set aside a mutually agreeable time and place to talk.

2. Define the problem, using good speaking and listening skills and owning your role from the start.

3. Generate all possible solutions in writing.

4. Evaluate the pros and cons of each alternative.

5. Decide on a solution in a spirit of collaboration and compromise, and write it down.

6. Decide how to implement the solution, building in any "cues" you can as reminders of what you've agreed to do.

Problem Solving Worksheet
Problem: Mary wants Tom to stop going fishing Sundays and wants him to spend time with her. She nags him about this, and he resents that. Write some consequences for your relationship

Consequences for the Relationship

Possible solutions   Pros   Cons

1.

2.

Alcohol Always Lied to Me

I Drank for Courage... and woke up night after night horrified.

I Drank for Sophistication... and became crude.

I Drank to find Peace... and ignited a war within myself.

I Drank to be Friendly... and became argumentative and nasty.

I Drank to be Sexy... and turned people off.

I Drank so that I could Relate to Others... and I babbled.

I Drank to put down Loneliness... and found myself retreating more and more into my shell.

I Drank to Relax... and woke up tense.

I Drank to be Entertaining... and became an obnoxious clown.

I Drank to Live More Fully... and contemplated suicide.

I Drank for Adventure... and discovered disaster.

I Drank to be more Honest... and insulted my friends.

I Drank to Quiet my Nerves... and woke up with hangover jangles.

I Drank to Feel Better... and ended up sick and throwing up.

I Drank to have Fun... and passed out in the middle of the party.

I Drank to Pep Myself Up... and ended up exhausted.

I Drank to feel Successful... a Big Shot... but ended up a failure.

I Drank for Security... and became afraid of my shadow.

I Drank to Feel Better about Myself... and ended up hating me.

I Drank to prove I could handle Alcohol and ended up knowing it controlled me.

A Friend said…"But surely, now that you've been Sober awhile, it would take a lot of alcohol to put you back in that condition." **"Just One Drink," I Answered!**

Chapter 3

In Search of the Black Family
The Relationship of Parenting

It is a well known fact in the Black community that we rear our daughters and spoil our sons. We do not teach our sons to be responsible and take care of their family. What usually happens is that our sons take on the role of man of the house. They become jealous of sharing their mother's affection with another male; their goal is to keep all men away from their mothers. They are often very vocal about their mom becoming involved romantically with another man. If a woman does become involved with a man and he is an alcoholic and abuses his mom, the male child will often come to his mom's defense physically. This creates a dangerous and volatile triad if the son feels the need to protect his mom. There are few men with the people skills and self-worth to take a secondary role and allow the child or children to bond with him. The other danger of in surrogate male partners and step dads is if the mother has a young girl. They will often fondle or touch the child in a sexual manner and threaten to harm the mom if the child tells.

There are some men who connect with women just to have sex with their daughter. In my counseling practice of thirty years, I found a lot of incest in families. In most cases the mother is too trusting and leaves the girl alone with the male. Girls are naturally playful and innocently sexual. Males may interpret this as seducing them and the sex act gets started and continues for years until the girl either gets pregnant or moves away from the home.

Most girls are not raped or sexually violated by a stranger. They usually know the perpetrator well. It is usually a brother, step dad, father, uncle, grand father or close friend of the family. Incest is defined as sexual relations with a family member. We rarely talk about that in the black community; however, it happens at an alarming rate. Mothers do not blame your daughter if this happens. Blame yourself; you are the one who is supposed to protect your daughter. It is not the daughter's role to look out for and protect the mother. There are many mothers who are in competition with their daughters, they are afraid to grow up and get old. They are jealous because their daughter is beautiful or have a nice figure.

All girls need more than one mom, in case one is an alcoholic like my mom and plenty of mentors (surrogate family) like the teachers I had who inspired me to get an education. Children today have to compete with their mom. The mothers refuse to grow up; they have long nails, chew gum, and keep their hair looking good, their face and body looking good, while their daughter struggles with low self-esteem trying to compete with them. Motherhood is a noble profession; however, there are few moms who want to sacrifice themselves and their life to build up the self-esteem of their daughters.

The other issue we need to address is our boys; there is no one to teach our boys how to become a man. The boys want two diamond ear rings in both ears, a cell phone in their hand and they cannot spell or read. They will watch television and all sports; however, they will argue with the mom, who is often single, and young to convince her they know how to read, while they take time to listen to the latest rap song for four hours. Boys learn early how to manipulate and disrespect women from the music they hear. Most of the music young men play today, is disrespectful of Black women and Black womanhood. It calls them "hoes, bitches, mother fuckers and any word that they can think of that is less than human. When I grew up, my brothers could only say yes "mam" and no 'mam" to my mom or my grand mom. My father did not allow anything else. Families stayed together then, my father was the head of the family, even though my mom worked two jobs and brought home the money. My father brought his money home, when he could find work, often as a migrant, picking fruit or vegetables in Pensacola or South Florida. After he paid the bills, he would buy a bottle of soda and share with the family.

My father sold everything, from snow cones to moon shine whiskey; which landed him an eighteen month stay in prison. After his stay in prison when I was age 15, he came back into our family and assumed his role as head of household as if he had never left. My father was a strict disciplinarian. At that time of my life, I thought he was the meanest person alive. We could not lean our greasy heads against the wall, if we stained the wall; he made us clean it right away. We all had to sit and eat dinner together at six in the afternoon, we could not talk with food in our mouths, we had to put our left hand in our lap and eat with our right hand. Whenever, my mom ate with her hands, an African custom, she learned in Alabama, my dad would correct her and she would leave the table, other times she would remain at the table if she wanted to eat with the family. My father spent time with both my brothers. He insisted that they read and do their homework. There are no dads in the homes today to guide, or insist that Black boys learn how to read.

The sad fact is that most Black boys are illiterate. They cannot spell or read; they can rap but they cannot read. Our boys are joining gangs at an alarming rate. When I was young there was no need for us to be in a gang. Family members looked out for each other. My older sister and my male cousin kept people from beating up on me. Today the boys join gangs they say to protect themselves. They would rather sell drugs and pimp women than go to college or get a job. We have failed our Black boys. We must insist that they read for one hour each day. In the 50's and 60's, Black families were still intact. Black men worked, stayed married to their wives and were a role model in the home for boys. If a boy got a girl pregnant in the south, especially in Pensacola Florida, where I grew up, the father insisted that he marry the girl. The intention was to let the community know and have the girl know that she thought enough about herself to have the man marry her. It was frowned upon for a girl to have a child out of wed lock.

Boys were made to realize that having illegitimate children was wrong. There was unpleasant community pressure if a boy got a girl pregnant and had no intention to marry her. It was a big thing for a child to know "who was his daddy." So many boys today have never seen and do not know who their daddy is. This is a tragedy for the self-esteem and positive self-identity for our Black boys. Mother rear your sons, find a daddy for them or a big brother who has a career they can respect and emulate. As a race of people we have strayed from our original close walk with Jesus, as to how we are to conduct ourselves, how we are to treat other Blacks (with respect and speak to them); take care of our elders, take care of the children in our village, protect the property of our neighbors, date and marry people of our race. Many of our young men are having babies by black women, but living with and marrying women of other races. When we disrespect others of our race, we disrespect ourselves, because we are an active participant.

As parents, we have failed our children by refusing to set standards of what is right and wrong behavior for them. Many of us want to be a pal or friend to our children. We are afraid to grow old; so we act and behave their age. We curse, yell, behave on their level, drink alcohol in front of, and with them, smoke marijuana in front of and with them. We dress inappropriately in front of our children, have male friends who disrespect us in front of our child; who often have sexual relations with the girl child with the mother's permission, because she leaves her alone with the male. In the cases where drugs are involved, I have known mothers who let men have sex with their daughters as young as age four, in exchange for drugs. Many of our children have to parent themselves, because there is no dad in the home, and the mom is out prostituting, selling and using drugs, or enjoying herself.

Another trend today is grandparents taking care of their grand children. Because, the father of the latest child does not want to take care of the other man's baby. Most times, it is the mom, who wants to start a new life. Another trend is, children being taken from parents, by Child Protective Services and placed into a foster home, because the parent whipped the child with a belt and left a scar, or the mom was fighting with her male companion, and the child heard or saw the abuse. We can still discipline our children we just cannot cause injury to their body. I will do a one day parenting class for free, through my non profit, Our Place Center of Self-Esteem, if I am contacted, 619-262-9951.

MOTHERS REAR YOUR SONS, HELP THEM TO BE EMOTIONALLY AND FINANCIALLY INDEPENDENT

PROBLEM
1. Low Self Esteem
2. Leadership Vacuum (fear)
3. Self-Confidence (lack of courage)
4. Things/People we Idolize
5. Wanting to be the Perfect Mother (well liked)
6. Control and Domination

SOLUTION
1. Self-Esteem, Love and Accept Yourself - Love Rightly.
2. Find and Create Appropriate Role Models.
3. Self-Confidence. Have courage to take a stand for the only person who believes in them; let them be God inspired.
4. Give up Control of your Child (Let Go and Let God Take Over)
5. Teach him the value of money (don't give him everything he wants).
6. Teach him to save money (you start a savings account for him with his allowance).
7. Don't allow yourself to be manipulated by sweet words (say them to yourself).
8. Role Models - Place him in the presence of males making money; actively seek them.

THE OLD PATHS

I liked the old paths, when
Moms were at home.
Dads were at work.
Brothers went into the army.
And sisters got married BEFORE having children.
Crime did not pay; hard work did;
and people knew the difference.
Moms could cook; Dads would work;
Children would behave.
Husbands were loving; wives were supportive; and
Children were polite.
Women wore the jewelry; and men wore the pants.
Women looked like ladies; Men looked like gentlemen;
and children looked decent.
People loved the truth, and hated a lie;
they came to church to get IN, Not to get OUT.
Hymns sounded Godly; Sermons sounded helpful;
Rejoicing sounded normal; and crying sounded sincere.
Cursing was wicked; Drinking was evil; and divorce was
unthinkable. America was beautiful; And God was
welcome!
 We read the Bible in public; Prayed in school;
 and preached from house to house.
 To be called an American was worth dying for;
 To be called a Christian was worth living for;
 To be called a traitor was a shame!
 Sex was a personal word.
 Homosexual was an unheard of word,
 And abortion was an illegal word.
 Preachers preached because they had a message;
 And Christians rejoiced because they had the VICTORY!
 Preachers preached from the Bible;
 Singers sang from the heart;
 And sinners turned to the Lord to be SAVED!

A new birth meant a new life; Salvation meant a changed life; following Christ led to eternal life.
Being a preacher meant you proclaimed the word of God;
Being a deacon meant you would serve the Lord;
Being a Christian meant you would live for Jesus;
And being a sinner meant someone was praying for you.
Laws were based on the Bible; Homes read the Bible; and Churches taught the Bible. Preachers were more interested in new converts, than new clothes and new cars. God was worshipped; Christ was exalted; and the Holy Spirit was respected. Church was where you found Christians on the Lord's Day, Rather than in the garden , on the creek bank, on the golf course or being entertained somewhere else, I still like the old paths the best.   Vivian Dreessen

The Awakening

"One single grateful thought raised to Heaven is the most perfect prayer."

"True prayer is not only expressed by your tongue but by your thoughts and actions as well. Synchronize all three and your prayer will be answered"

A time comes in your life when you finally get it ... when, in the midst of all your fears and insanity, you stop dead in your tracks and somewhere the voice inside your head cries out "ENOUGH!" Enough fighting, crying or struggling to hold onto.

And like a child quieting down after a blind tantrum, your sobs begin to subside, you shudder once or twice, you blink back your tears and begin to look at the world through new eyes. This is your awakening.

You realize it's time to stop hoping and waiting for something to change or for happiness, safety, and security to come galloping over the next horizon. You come to terms with the fact that you are neither Prince Charming nor Cinderella. And that, in the real world, there aren't always fairy-tale endings or beginnings, for that matter.

And that any guarantee of "happily ever after" must begin with you and in the process, a sense of serenity is born of acceptance.
You awaken to the fact that you are not perfect and that not everyone will always love, appreciate, or approve of who or what you are and that's OK. They are entitled to their own views and opinions.

And you learn the importance of loving and championing yourself ... and in the process, a sense of new-found confidence is born of self-approval.
You stop complaining and blaming other people for the things they did to you (or didn't do for you) and you learn that the only thing you can really count on is the unexpected.

You learn that people don't always say what they mean or mean what they say, and that not everyone will always be there for you, and that it's not always about you.

So you learn to stand on your own and to take care of yourself, and in the process, a sense of safety and security is born of self-reliance.
You stop judging and pointing fingers and you begin to accept people as they are and overlook their shortcomings and human frailties ... and in the process, a sense of peace and contentment is born of forgiveness.

You realize that much of the way you view yourself and the world around you is as a result of all the messages and opinions that have been ingrained into your psyche.

And you begin to sift through all the junk you've been fed about how you should behave, how you should look, how much you should weigh, what you should wear, what you should do for a living, how much money you should make, what you should drive, how and where you should live, who you should marry, the importance of having and raising children, and what you owe your parents, family, and friends.

You learn to open up to new worlds and different points of view. And you begin reassessing and redefining who you are and what you stand for.

You learn the differences between wanting and needing and you begin to discard the doctrines and values you've outgrown, or should never have bought into to begin with ... and in the process, you learn to go with your instincts.

You learn that it is truly in giving that we receive. And that there is power and glory in creating and contributing and you stop maneuvering through life merely as a "consumer" looking for your next fix. You learn that principles such as honesty and integrity are not outdated ideals of a bygone era but the mortar that holds together the foundation upon which you must build a life.

You learn that you don't know everything, it's not your job to save the world and that you can't teach a pig to sing. You learn to distinguish between guilt and responsibility and the importance of setting boundaries and learning to say NO.

You learn that the only cross to bear is the one you choose to carry and that martyrs get burned at the stake. Then you learn about love. How to love, how much to give in love, when to stop giving and when to walk away.

You learn to look at relationships as they really are and not as you would have them be. You stop trying to control people, situation, and outcomes.

You learn that alone does not mean lonely. You also stop working so hard at putting your feelings aside, smoothing things over and ignoring your needs.

You learn that feelings of entitlement are perfectly OK, and that it is your right to want things and to ask for the things you want ... and that sometimes it is necessary to make demands.

You come to the realization that you deserve to be treated with love, kindness, sensitivity, and respect ... and you won't settle for less. And you learn that your body really is your temple. And you begin to care for it and treat it with respect. You begin to eat a balanced diet, drink more water, and take more time to exercise.
You learn that being tired fuels doubt, fear, and uncertainty and so you take more time to rest.
And, just as food fuels the body, laughter fuels our soul. So you take more time to laugh and to play.

You learn that, for the most part, you get in life what you believe you deserve ... and that much of life truly is a self-fulfilling prophecy. You learn anything worth achieving is worth working for and wishing for something to happen is different from working toward making it happen. More importantly, you learn that in order to achieve success you need direction, discipline, and perseverance.
You also learn that no one can do it all alone ... and that it's OK to risk asking for help.

You learn the only thing you must truly fear is the greatest robber baron of all: FEAR itself. You learn to step right into and through your fears because you know that whatever happens you can handle it and to give in to fear is to give away the right to live life on your own terms.

And you learn to fight for your life and not to squander it living under a cloud of impending doom.
You learn that life isn't always fair; you don't always get what you think you deserve, and that bad things sometimes happen to unsuspecting, good people.
On these occasions you learn not to personalize things. You learn that God isn't punishing you or failing to answer your prayers. It's just life happening.

And you learn to deal with evil in its most primal state ... the ego. You learn that negative feelings such as anger, envy, and resentment must be understood and redirected or they will suffocate the life out of you and poison the universe that surrounds you. You learn to admit when you are wrong and build bridges instead of walls.

You learn to be thankful and to take comfort in many of the simple things we take for granted, things that millions of people upon the earth can only dream about: a full refrigerator, clean running water, a soft warm bed, a long hot shower.

Slowly you begin to take responsibility for yourself by yourself and you make yourself a promise to never betray yourself and to never, ever settle for less than your heart's desire. Hang a wind chime outside your window so you can listen to the wind.
Keep smiling, keep trusting, and stay open to every wonderful possibility.

Finally, with courage in your heart, take a stand, a deep breath, and begin to design as best you can the life you want to live. Choice by Choice. ~Virginia Marie Swift

The Rugged Roads of Life

Life is an ever increasing spiral,
On the path to human perfection.
It matters not the hue of your skin,
The color of your eyes, not the color of your hair.
For self-mastery is an inner process,
That happens each time you overcome an obstacle.
No one can ever determine,
The depth of your learning experience.
So continue on your journey, to overcome
Your stiffest challenges,
For no one will ever know, the depths of your overcoming.
Continue to strive for excellence in every thing you do.
For the path to fulfillment and happiness
Is the rugged road of life?
Ida Greene

Home Rules for Family Members

If you sleep on it	Make it up
If you wear it	Hang it up
If you drop it	Pick it up
If you eat out of it	Put it in the sink
If you step on it	Wipe it off
If you open it	Close it
If you empty it	Fill it up
If it rings	Answer it
If it howls	Feed it
If it cries	Love it

Things We Do to Get Attention

Check those things you do to get attention. Circle the one thing you do most often to get attention.

a. ____ Do dumb things
b. ____ Act sick.
c. ____ Do things extra well so people will notice.
d. ____ Don't talk.
e. ____ Pout.
f. ____ Pick on someone.
g. ____ Pretend you are bored.
h. ____ Cry.
i. ____ Put others down.
j. ____ Other

What did you learn about your pattern of connecting and interacting with others?

Do you get attention in a negative, dramatic fashion; state how you get attention if it is not listed?

_____

Please create a plan for getting attention in more positive ways than those listed above. Describe your plan below.

_____
_____
_____
_____
_____

Twelve Steps to Create Intimacy in a Relationship

1. Learn to identify your own thoughts, feelings and behaviors.
2. Begin to own them as distinctly and separately yours, not confused with someone else's.
3. Begin to explore my own spirit, mind and body, gently and lovingly..
4. Be willing to tell my partner/friend what I like and what I dislike.
5. Tell my partner/friend, out loud, what I want, clearly and specifically.
6. Say "yes" to my partner/friend when I mean "yes", and "no" when I mean "no".
7. Say, and come to believe, that my needs and wants are important, and that my partner's/ friend's are important.
8. Become comfortable with the idea that today's "no" may become "Yes" tomorrow for both my partner/friend's and me.
9. Say "no" in such a way that my partner's /friend's self-esteem is not diminished.
10. Hear my partner's/friend's "no" in a way that my own self-esteem doesn't suffer.
11. Be willing to look for alternatives and compromise when there is disagreement on important issues.
12. Help my partner to behave assertively with me.

                    Susan Griffin

"We Are What We Think. All That We Are Arises With Our Thoughts. With Our Thoughts We Make The World."
    ~Gautama Buddha (written around 80 B.C)

How to Stir Up a Spirit of Hope and Joy Inside You

I am a fun loving, intelligent lady who has a plan for her life. I am committed to make the world a better place for those less fortunate than myself. I am a positive person who knows how to make things happen for myself and others. At this point in my life I am here to do God's will, to spread LOVE in the universe.

To me, everything is a lesson to be learned. Every problem or challenge I have experienced has made me stronger, wiser and has taught me to put my trust 100% in God. Knowing that everyone is doing the best they can at this moment in time. Rather than judge or make others wrong I just keep moving, until I find someone with shared values. Life is a journey to be enjoyed and people are fascinating. No one is an island unto themselves. Do not be afraid to show your weaknesses or expose your fears.

I love my relationship with my family, with the abused children I serve through my non profit organization, myself and people. I love people. I find them complex and fascinating. I love life and living. I thank God every day for my mind, good health, air to breath, the beautiful blue sky and another day to be in the land of the living.

Words Of Wisdom
Things I Learned From Life and Living

1. Give people more than they expect and do it cheerfully.
2. Marry a man/woman you love to talk to. As you get older their conversational skills will be as important as any other.
3. Don't believe all you hear, spend all you have or sleep all you want.
4. When you say "I love you," mean it.
5. When you say "I'm sorry," look the person in the eye.
6. Be engaged at least six months before you get married.
7. Believe in love at first sight.
8. Never laugh at anyone's dreams. People who don't have dreams don't have
9. much.
10. Love deeply and passionately. You might get hurt but it's the only way to
11. live life.
12. In disagreements, fight fairly. No name calling.
13. Don't judge people by their relatives.
14. Talk slowly, but think quickly.
15. When someone asks you a question you don't want to answer, smile and Ask, "Why do you want to know?
16. Remember that great love and great achievements involve great risk.
17. Say "bless you," when you hear someone sneeze.
18. When you lose, don't lose the lesson.

19. Remember the three R's: Respect for self, Respect for others and responsibility for all your actions.
20. Don't let a dispute injure a great friendship.
21. When you realize you've made a mistake, take immediate action to control it.
22. Smile when picking up the phone. The caller will hear it in your voice.
23. Spend some time alone.

Ida Greene, PhD

The Paradox of Our Age is:

We have taller buildings, but shorter tempers, wider freeways, but narrow viewpoints; we spend more, but have less; we buy more, but enjoy it less.

We have bigger houses and small families; more conveniences, but less time. We have more degrees, but less sense; more knowledge, but less judgment; more experts, but more problems; more medicine, but less wellness. We drink too much, smoke too much, spend too recklessly, laugh too little, drive too fast, get too angry too quickly, stay up too late, get up too tired, read too seldom, watch T.V. too much, and pray too seldom.

We have multiplied our possessions but reduced our values. We talk too much, love too seldom and lie too often. We've learned how to make a living, but not a life; we've added years to life, but not life to years. We've been all the way to the moon and back, but have trouble crossing the street to meet the new neighbor.

We've conquered outer space but not inner space; we've done larger things, but not better things; we've cleared up the air, but polluted the soul; we've split the atom, but not our prejudice; we write more, but learn less; plan more; but accomplish less. We've learned to rush, but not to wait; we have higher incomes; but lower morals; more food but less appeasement; more acquaintances, but fewer friends; more effort, but less success. We build more computers to hold more information, to produce more copies than ever, but have less communication; we've become long on quantity, but short on quality.

These are the times of fast foods and slow digestion; tall men and short characters. There are the times of world peace, but domestic warfare; more leisure and less fun; more kinds of food, but less nutrition. These are days of two incomes, but more divorce; of fancier houses, but broken homes. These are days of quick trips, disposable diapers, throwaway morality, one-night stands, overweight bodies and ills that do everything from cheer, to quiet, to kill. It is a time when there is much in the show window and nothing in the stockroom. Indeed this is all true!

Chapter 4

You and Your RelationshipWith Money

How your money blueprint is formed. Your "money blueprint" is a preset program or way of being in relation to your money. Your financial blueprint is composed of your thoughts, feelings and actions in the arena of money. These are based on your "inner world" your thoughts. They lead to your results, which are based in your outer world. So how do you get your money blueprint? Your money blueprint consists primarily of the "mental programming" you received in your past, as a young child. The primary sources of this conditioning were your parents, siblings, friends, authority figures, religious leaders, media and your culture. Some cultures have a certain way of thinking and dealing with money while in other cultures it's completely different?

A child does not come out of the womb with a particular attitude about money. A child is "taught" how to think about and act in relation to money. You were "taught" how to think about and handle money; you took on this mental conditioning at an early age. You played this tape in your head repeatedly and it became ingrained in your being, because you replayed it over and over in your head. Now it will be for the rest of your life, until you reprogram your mind.

The 3 Primary Methods of Conditioning
1. Verbal programming: what you "heard" when you were young.
2. Modeling: what you "saw" when you were young.
3. Specific incidents: what you experienced when you were young.

Childhood Verbal Programming on Money
What did you hear about money, wealth and rich people when you were growing up, did you hear?
Money is the root of all evil.
Rich people are greedy.
You have to work hard to make money.
You can't be rich and spiritual.
Money doesn't buy happiness.
The rich get richer and the poor get poorer.

The Power of Prosperity Thoughts

Prosperity thoughts are for everyone. Whoever you are and wherever you may be, you can receive greater prosperity. Jesus said, "Seek first his kingdom and his righteousness, and all these things shall be yours as well" (Matthew 6:33). A fuller understanding of the law of creation reveals that this "righteousness" is not conforming to a particular religious belief, but holding right thoughts regardless of creed, dogma, or religious form of any description. Think right thoughts and you will demonstrate prosperity. Cultivate the habit of thinking about abundance everywhere. When Jesus was shown the piece of money with the image of Caesar upon it, He said "Render to Caesar the things that are Caesar's and to God the things that are God's" (Mark 12:17). He did not mean to make a great separation between the two, as if they were at odds. The lesson is one of right relation: be responsible in both your material and spiritual matters.

Remember that prosperity does not wholly depend on money or environment. Poverty is a condition brought about by certain ideas ruling in consciousness (your mind). When you change your ideas, your condition will change in spite of the environment. Persons who suddenly come into riches without the mind set of riches as a "balance wheel" soon part with their money. Those who are born into riches usually have plenty, though they may never make an effort to earn a dollar themselves. This is because the idea of plenty is so interwoven in their thoughts that it is a part of their lives. They have no belief of a situation or condition where the necessities of life were lacking. Children born into luxury give no place in their thoughts to the possibility of poverty. They cannot imagine being without money or not having their needs met.

You may ask if I advocate, the accumulation of riches, I say No. I advocate the accumulation and use of rich ideas that can produce money. Rich ideas are ideas of service: They are constructive, useful ideas that produce good; these ideas promote the well-being of humankind. People who have rich ideas have confidence in a providing power. They may not be in possession of dollars, but they know that their undertakings have merit and that the money to carry them forward will be forthcoming. True prosperity is confidence in a Divine power (a resource) that is always ready to meet our needs.

Substance in the form of money is given to us for constructive uses. It should neither be hoarded nor foolishly wasted. In finding freedom from the thought of hoarding, many people go to the opposite extreme of extravagant spending. Money should be used to increase and draw forth good for ourselves and others. It is good to pay your obligations. It is good to have money on hand for education, travel, hospitality, developing industries for the good of humanity, furthering spiritual work, helping others build true and useful lives, and any other constructive purpose or activity.

In conserving money, you should keep in mind the necessity of having a constructive motive behind your action. Money saved with the fearful thought of a "rainy day" or for a prolonged season of lack and suffering will more than likely have to be used for that purpose. Fear tends to attract that which is feared. Money that is hoarded with a miserly thought cannot bring you blessings. Money that is conserved as an "opportunity fund" will bring its increase of good. Those who have fretful thoughts of accumulation that is dominant in the financial world are inviting trouble, because their thoughts are accompanied by a fear of loss of riches. Fearful holding of money will make you insecure. Worldly prosperity that is not based on the source of riches, eventually leads to disaster. Being rich is not a sin. It is the worship of money. The sin of being rich is the love of money: which is material selfishness and leads to soul starvation. "For what does it profit a man to gain the whole world and forfeit his life?" (Mark 8:36).

    Some people think that all they have to do is to sit down and hold thoughts of abundant supply and it will come without any effort. This is limiting the law of thought. The law must be fulfilled in manifestation as well as in thought. Cultivating ideas of abundance is the first step in the process to create money. The second step is being alert and doing whatever is yours to do, cheerfully and competently. This fulfills the law, which says, "The earth is the Lord's and the fullness thereof" (Psalm 24:1). Jesus did not own any land, had "nowhere to lay his head" (Matthew 8:20), and yet he was wealthy. He understood that what He needed was to ask. Jesus demonstrated that He was the Son of God. From the invisible ethers, He handed out food for thousands. He was inherently rich. He proved that the earth belongs, in all its fullness, to God and that the righteous children of God are in possession of everything. When Jesus said" "Do not be anxious about your life, what you shall eat, nor about your body, what you shall put on" (Luke. 12:22), He was giving a lesson concerning negative thoughts, anxiety, and fear of future lack. The assurance of God's all providing care as illustrated by the lilies of the field and by the sparrows is striking and convincing. Your anxious thoughts must be eliminated and replaced with thoughts of unlimited resources, and then you will experience the fulfillment of the divine law of prosperity.

A Prosperity Lesson, Charles Fillmore

(To receive the full benefits of this lesson, first read the noted passage from your Bible.) In the Old Testament, (2 Kings 4:1-7), is a prosperity lesson.
A "widow" is one who has lost sight of her support. The Divine idea of God as His abundance is our support.

The two children represent the bondage of thought of debt. Elisha is Divine understanding and power. The "house" is consciousness. The "pot of oil" is faith in spiritual Substance. The "neighbors" are external states of mind, and their "empty vessels" are thoughts of lack. To "go in and shut the door" is to enter the inner consciousness. This is to be followed by using words of Gods' abundance, pouring all places of apparent lack full of manifest substance. Each "vessel," or need, is to be filled in thought with the consciousness of Spirit Abundance. Affirm that your every obligation is met and that a surplus remains, equal to all your needs. This is all to be done in the mind, every step being carried forward in your imagination exactly as if it were occurring in the without. Then hold to the Divine Law of fulfillment. "Having done all to stand" (Ephesians 6:13).

You may not be able to fill all the vessels with oil at the first attempt, but let your faith increase day by day. Keep right at the problem until you prove it. Do not let a single empty thought exist in your mind, but fill all thoughts with words of plenty! Plenty! If your pocketbook is empty, fill it with a thought like this" "I pour into you the bounty of God, my father, who supplies all my wants." If your rooms are empty, say: "I deny this appearance, let prosperity be manifest in you." If you want to open up new avenues of work, say: "The Spirit of Prosperity is now active in me and in all my affairs, and I am successful in all my undertakings." Be just and honest in all your ways. Do not try to get something for nothing, but give value received for everything. Unity, March, 1910

Never think of yourself as poor or needy, nor talk about "hard times" and the necessity of economy. Do not think how little you have; think how much you have. Associate with people who are holding prosperous thoughts and cultivate the optimistic side of every question. Take things by the smooth handle. Look on the bright side. Trust the goodness and power of God to right every wrong; help to make the Divine Law operative in the world by declaring your faith in it. "Let your light…shine" (Matthew 5:16). "Seek first his kingdom and his righteousness, and all these things shall be yours as well" (Matthew. 6:33).

On Money and Prosperity

As Deepak Chopra reminds us: "Practicing the Law of Giving is very simple: if you want joy, give joy to others; if you want love, learn to give love; if you want attention and appreciation, learn to give attention and appreciation; if you want material affluence, help others to become materially affluent. In fact, the easiest way to get what you want is to help others get what they want. This principle works equally well for individuals, corporations, societies, and nations. If you want to be blessed with all the good things in life, learn to silently bless everyone with all of the good things in life."

Have you ever wondered why one person walking down a dark alley at night will get mugged while the previous person goes by untouched? Bad things may happen to apparently "good" people and good things happen to seemingly "bad" people all based upon the level of energy that they are vibrating at the time. You are like a radio tower that is constantly transmitting a certain frequency into the Universe. Your thoughts and feelings create an energetic vibration that is sent out into the world. This vibration is then reflected back to you by the Universe, producing physical results in your personal world. What you send out is exactly what you get back our body's actually send out a specific frequency of energy, which if its positive will magnetizes back to us similar vibration experiences (such as great opportunities, positive-minded people, wealthy clients, big bank accounts, etc.) On the other hand, when we are sending out the energy of doubt, frustration, or fear, we tend to magnetize very difficult and challenging experiences that make us suffer endlessly. In order to manifest what you want you must consistently emit high frequency of thoughts, feelings and vibrations about your life.

Whatever you continuously focus your attention on, is what you will manifest in your life. By nature, you are a manifesting machine who cannot stop manifesting what you are focusing on. We attract what shows up in our thoughts, feelings, attitudes and everyday energetic patterns. The fact is if you are able to keep your mind on what you Really Want twenty four hours a day, you'll manifest exactly that. These are ancient secrets to remain focused to achieve this spiritual strength needed to obtain your monumental feat and have a high and consistent *Manifesting Vibration*.

A Manifesting vibration is the frequency of energy your body and mind vibrate at, which tend to attract or repel the thing you desire. The highest energy vibrations we have are when we are full of joy, gratitude, excitement, and love. If you knew how to remain in these vibrations twenty hours a day, you could manifest anything you desire. When you do so, you will receive what you want easier than ever before. Once you know the secrets to keeping your mind focused "only" on what you really "want" twenty four hours a day, your hearts greatest desires are sure to come.

How to Avoid Money Anxieties and Worries

Money itself has become the symbol of world wealth. We have learned to associate some of our most potent and debilitating emotions to a scarcity of this money: anxiety, frustration, fears, insecurity, worry, anger, humiliation, overwhelms, depression, to name a few. I bring this up simply because I wonder if you're at all like me. For years without realizing it; I focused on "true" success. I became successful (that is, I managed to consistently expand the quality of my life) in my relationships, my physical health, my relationship with God, and my intellectual and mental abilities.

I wanted to prove to myself that I could create growth in the financial world as I had in other areas of my life. It did not make me money hungry; however, it created a greater appreciation in me for life and makes me want to share my experiences with others. I realize now that earning more money doesn't create financial freedom. Financial freedom is a learned behavior and a state of mind.

Learning from your own experience can be an expensive lesson. As a result, I have begun to observe some of the top financial people in this country, to see how they evaluate and make financial decisions. Most people have mixed associations with money. Whether this association is conscious or subconscious, it can affect our relationship with money. If you do not clear up your faulty money associations, long term financial success will delude you. Turning your faulty money associations around is the best financial insurance you can have. In order to have lasting financial wealth, you must change the associations you make to money in your nervous system. You cannot have lasting wealth if you link pain and pleasure to having it.

Tell yourself, it is fun, joyous, loving and Godly for you to have money. What would it take for you know that you are truly wealthy? Would you have to earn a million dollars a year? Have the biggest car or home? Or do you feel wealthy because you know your life is making a difference on the planet? We associate so much pain and pleasure to money. We give money a lot of power to control our lives. Money is a resource and a convenience. It is a process of exchanging one thing of value for another.

We have negative or mixed associations as to what having excess money means. Most people do not achieve what they want in life because they have mixed associations about acquiring or having money. Money is a prime example of this. People say, I want money because it provides freedom, the chance to do things for my family, contribute to my friends, community, society at large and a change to have nice things and opportunities.

There are many negative beliefs surrounding money, some of them are: "In order to have money you have to work very hard" (i.e. pain), or "you have to spend all your time making money," "you can't be spiritual," or people will judge you." When we have these mixed associations surrounding money, our brain does not know whether it should move ahead or pull back. So most of us settle for an amount of money that is not abundant - it is just enough to "get by". These negative or mixed associations literally destroy our opportunities for developing long-term wealth.

Failing to develop a consistent strategy or plan for creating long-term wealth is a tragedy. You need a plan to attract money, a plan to manage and invest your money; and a plan on how to enjoy your money so that your brain links pleasure to money and says, I want more of this."

I define financial independence as the point when you accumulate enough money so that the interest on the capital offers you an annual income and enables you to live at your present lifestyle, or better, for the rest of your life without ever working unless you choose to.

So the first step in developing your plan is to find out how much income you need annually to be financially free. For example, if a person needed $50,000 a year income, and they could earn interest on investments of approximately 8%, they would need to accumulate $625,000. That may sound like a lot, but using some simple strategies and the power of compound growth, anyone with a small amount of money to invest can develop this kind of wealth and freedom.

Once you know your goal. the next step is to develop an effective investment philosophy, which is a set of distinctions you will use to make decisions about your future investment choices. You must determine in what to invest. There are three points to making good investment choices: First, you need to get exposure and educate yourself on investments. It is very important to learn all the different types of investments.

Second, invest in something you enjoy, so that no matter what happens, you'll feel great about your investment. When I bought my Home, I thought, "Even if it doesn't go up in value, for me it's going to be worth it, because I enjoy owning this and living here."

Third, invest in something you understand. It always amazes my mind to see a brain surgeon or a dentist invests in oil wells which they know nothing about.

Fourth key, always invest, focusing on long-term success. Most people make money owning their own homes because it's a long-term investment. People who lost money in the real estate market because of the current excitement which pushed the price up.

To have an effective investment philosophy, is to buy real value when it is unpopular, and sell when it is popular. Buy something that for a variety of reasons is unpopular today, than find a way to improve it and make it popular , so you can sell it when it is popular and take a great profit. Most importantly, keep your emotions out of your investment plan. Remember, building wealth is a strategy for what to invest in and when. Building wealth is based on your ability to manage your emotions about your investments. You have to be able to stifle the desire for instantaneous gratification, and have courage when other people are fearful about money. If you want to be poor, here is a simple formula: Buy out of greed, and sell when you are fearful. That's a guaranteed way to lose big money. Selling out of fear is the wrong time to sell... When people think they are about to lose their investment, often they will do anything to get rid of what they have. This is usually a mistake.

Get clear on what financial independence means to you. Develop a clear cut plan and philosophy that supports you in achieving this goal. Take your first actions in enacting this plan within 90 days as an absolute maximum. Remember, knowing what to do is not enough. Do what you know. I look forward to hearing the story of your personal and financial success. Remember to take charge of your financial destiny, enjoy your life, and live it with passion and love for humanity.

What is Financial Security?

Where you put your money determines your financial destiny. It is the balance between what you put into something that's secure and it builds long term profits. The money you risk will determine more than anything your ultimate financial destiny.

1. Take out a piece of paper. Write down the words "financial independence" and for approximately five minutes, write down every word you associate to it. Next, do that with the word "wealth" and then the word "excess" (you may discover you have some negative associations to this one!).
2. Write down all the fears you have about what it would take for you to be financially independent, or any negative subconscious associations that didn't come up in step one of your homework.
3. Define how much money you need as an annual income that would support you in feeling totally financially free. An annual income that, if this money came in, you would only work because you wanted to, not because you had to.
4. Determine how much additional money you could put aside each month if you were committed to developing a savings to invest.
5. Make a list of all the reasons why having financial independence is a must for you, and all the reasons why you must have it now.

Thoughts to Ponder

ONE. Give people more than they expect and do it cheerfully...
TWO. Marry a man/woman you love to talk to. As you get older, their conversational skills will be as important as any other.
THREE. Don't believe all you hear, spend all you have or sleep all you want.
FOUR. When you say, "I love you," mean it.
FIVE. When you say, "I'm sorry," look the person in the eye.
SIX. Be engaged at least six months before you get married.
SEVEN. Believe in love at first sight.
EIGHT. Never laugh at anyone's dream. People who don't have dreams don't have much.
NINE. Love deeply and passionately. You might get hurt but it's the only way to live life completely.
TEN... In disagreements, fight fairly. No name calling.
ELEVEN. Don't judge people by their relatives.
TWELVE. Talk slowly but think quickly.
THIRTEEN. When someone asks you a question you don't want to answer, smile and ask, "Why do you want to know?"
FOURTEEN. Remember that great love and great achievements involve great risk.
FIFTEEN. Say "bless you" when you hear someone sneeze.
SIXTEEN. When you lose, don't lose the lesson.
SEVENTEEN. Remember the three R's: Respect for self; Respect for others; and Responsibility for all your actions.
EIGHTEEN. Don't let a little dispute injure a great friendship.
NINETEEN. When you realize you've made a mistake, take immediate steps to correct it.

TWENTY. Smile when you pick up the phone. The caller will hear it in your voice.
TWENTY-ONE. Spend some time alone.
Jafree Ozwald

Prayer Treatment for Right Employment

There is a place for me in the job market and I expect to find it.
It is the right place, the position for which I am both qualified and ready.
Within me as I speak is an intelligence that knows what my right job is, where it is, and when I will find it.
I call upon this power now to guide me in the right direction.
I release all anxiety and wait with confidence for my intuition to show me the next step to take.
I accept my right employment now.
I am open minded and willing to be guided by the Divine Mind of God.
Ida Greene

How to Develop Positive Thought Patterns

I have control of my thoughts and want them to follow positive patterns. Where I have fallen into negative thought habits, I will change them by remembering to reverse my negative reactions, one by one, until new habits are established. If fear arises, I will speak my faith. If I start to criticize someone, I will stop short and declare that God's love is more important than my opinion. God's love can heal us both. And I accept God's love now to support me in my determination to improve my thought patterns.

Ida Greene

The 15 Laws of Life

1. Love is the Law of Life
All love is expansion, all selfishness is contraction. Love is therefore the only law of life. He who loves lives, he who is selfish is dying. Therefore, love for love's sake, because it is law of life, just as you breathe to live.

2. It is Your Outlook That Matters
It is our own mental attitude, which makes the world what it is for us. Our thoughts make things beautiful, our thoughts make things ugly. The whole world is in our own minds. Learn to see things in the proper light.

3. Life is Beautiful
First, believe in this world - that there is meaning behind everything. Everything in the world is good, is holy and beautiful. If you see something evil, think that you do not understand it in the right light. Throw the burden on yourselves!

4. It is The Way You Feel
Feel like Christ and you will be a Christ; feel like Buddha and you will be a Buddha. It is feeling that is the life, the strength, the vitality, without which no amount of intellectual activity can reach God.

5. Set Yourself Free
The moment I have realized God sitting in the temple of every human body, the moment I stand in reverence before every human being and see God in him - that moment I am free from bondage, everything that binds vanishes, and I am free.

6. Don't Play the Blame Game
Condemn none: if you can stretch out a helping hand, do so. If you cannot, fold your hands, bless your brothers, and let them go their own way.

7. Help Others
If money helps a man to do good to others, it is of some value; but if not, it is simply a mass of evil, and the sooner it is got rid of the better.

8. Uphold Your Ideals
Our duty is to encourage every one in his struggle to live up to his own highest idea, and strive at the same time to make the ideal as near as possible to the Truth.

9. Listen to Your Soul
You have to grow from the inside out. None can teach you, none can make you spiritual. There is no other teacher but your own soul.

10. Be Yourself
The greatest religion is to be true to your own nature. Have faith in yourselves!

11. Nothing Is Impossible
Never think there is anything impossible for the soul. It is the greatest heresy to think so. If there is sin, this is the only sin - to say that you are weak, or others are weak

12. You Have the Power
All the powers in the universe are already ours. It is we who have put our hands before our eyes and cry that it is dark.

13. Learn Everyday
The goal of mankind is knowledge... now this knowledge is inherent in man. No knowledge comes from outside: it is all inside. What we say a man 'knows', should, in strict psychological language, be what he 'discovers' or 'unveils'; what man 'learns' is really what he discovers by taking the cover off his own soul, which is a mine of infinite knowledge.

14. Be Truthful
Everything can be sacrificed for truth, but truth cannot be sacrificed for anything.

15. Think Differently
All the differences in this world are of degree, and not of kind, because oneness is the secret of everything we are more alike than we are different. Swami Vivekananda

"Holding on to anger is like grasping a hot coal with the intent of throwing it at someone else; you are the one who gets burned." ~Buddha

You are like a radio tower that is constantly transmitting a certain frequency into the Universe. Your thoughts and feelings create an energetic vibration that is sent out into the world. This vibration is then reflected back to you by the Universe, (God) producing physical results in your personal world. The truth is that we are always creating something. Whether you are manifesting what *you want* or what you *do not want* depends on the level of your vibration. We are like manifesting magnets! We attract what mirrors our feelings and thinking patterns. So what we send out is *exactly* what we get back. For example, when we are full of joy, gratitude, or excitement, we tend to send out a high frequency energy, which in turn magnetizes back high frequency experiences. Like great opportunities, positive-minded people, wealthy clients, big bank accounts, etc. On the other hand, when we send out the energy of doubt, frustration, or fear, we tend to magnetize challenging experiences that we do not want. So all you need to do in order to be successful is to constantly emit high frequency vibrations which will attract your desires to you.

It is important to know that we are each born with the natural power to create our own reality. We do so everyday. The real question is.. are you creating what *you want*, or are you stuck in creating **what you do not want**? The truth is you are a manifesting machine. **You cannot stop manifesting. Whatever you are focusing on is what you will manifest.** If you are constantly thinking about how you wish you had a million dollars that's exactly what you will get. Once you learn how to train your mind to stay focused *only* on the thing you want to have, that experience will find its way into your life.

"Life is an adventure to be lived, not a problem to be solved." Osho

Abundance Attracting Qualities and Repelling Qualities

1. Honoring your worth and time/ Not honoring your worth and time.
2. Giving and receiving freely/ Not giving or being open to receiving.
3. Opening your heart/ Closing your heart.
4. Expecting the best to happen/ Worrying that the worst will happen.
5. Coming from your heart/ Getting into power struggles.
6. Doing your best/ Cutting corners.
7. Wanting everyone to succeed, cooperating/ Competing.
8. Focusing on how you can serve others/ Thinking only of what others will give you.
9. Telling yourself why you can succeed/ Telling yourself why you can't succeed.
10. Coming from your integrity/ Compromising your values and ideas.

11. Being aware and paying attention/ Operating on automatic
12. Applauding others' success/ Feeling threatened by others' success.
13. Embracing your challenges/ Choosing safety and comfort over growth.
14. Releasing things easily/ Hanging on to things.
15. Believe it's never too late, taking action on your dreams/ Think it's too late, giving up.

16. Giving yourself permission to be and do what you want/ Waiting for others to give you permission.
17. Believing your path is important/ Not believing in your path.

18. Doing what you love for your livelihood/ Working only for the money.
19. Detaching, surrender to your higher good/ Feeling needy, that you must have something.
20. Giving to other's prosperity/ Giving to other's need.

21. Doing your higher purpose activities first/ Putting off higher purpose activities until you have more time.
22. See yourself as the source of your abundance/ View others as the source of your abundance.

23. Believing in abundance/ Believing in scarcity.
24. Believing in yourself, self-confidence, self-love/ Worry, fears, doubts, self-criticism.
25. Clear intent and directed will/ Vague or undefined goals.
26. Following your joy/ Forcing yourself, creating "have to's" and should's".
27. Surrounding yourself with objects that reflect your aliveness/ Keeping objects that aren't tools to express your aliveness.

28. Expressing gratitude and thanks/ Feeling the world owes you.
29. Trusting in your ability to create abundance/ Worrying over finances.
30. Following your inner guidance/ ignoring inner guidance.
31. Looking for a winning solution for everyone/ Not caring if the other person wins.
32. Becoming your own authority/ Not believing in your inner wisdom

33. Measuring abundance as fulfilling your purpose and happiness/ Acknowledging abundance only by how much money you have.
34. Enjoying the process as much as the goal/ Doing things only for the goal...
35. Clear agreements/ Unspoken or vague expectations.
36. Thinking how far you have come/ Focusing on how far you have to go.

37. Speaking of abundance/ Talking about problems and lack.
38. Remembering past successes/ Remembering past failures.

39. Thinking in expanded, unlimited ways/ Thinking in limited ways.
40. Think of how you will create money/ Thinking of how you need money.
41. Focusing on what you love and want/ Focusing only on what you don't want.
42. Allowing yourself to have/ Feeling you don't deserve to have.

Chapter 5

Business Ownership,
Keys to Getting What You Want

Entrepreneurship is the new explosion in the Black Community. The essential step to get anything you want. Almost every week I receive emails from people who say they are stuck, confused, lost and need "help" to achieve their goals in life. As much as I can, I respond personally to those emails. There are a lot of reasons why people get frustrated or struggle in life. One of the most common reason is that some people are lazy and refuse to get started. Some people have big dreams but refuse to take the first steps to make them come true. Thinking about something will not cause it to happen.

One of Newton's laws says that for every action there is an equal reaction. Tony Robbins is famous for his observation that high achievers take massive action. They observe their results, adjust accordingly, and take more action. There is tremendous power in persistent, determined action. There is a famous phrase in the Bible that says the "truth shall set you free" and a key truth is that to achieve any goal, no matter what it is, some action, effort, work, activity, physical exertion is required and the activity must come "First". To achieve your goals, action is required. Often the required action is simple, easy and obvious.

Over my years as a coach, I've had conversations with people who want to reach ordinary sort of goals that a lot of other people have achieved. They want to save for retirement, start a business, travel the world, or do something that seemed difficult to them, but has been achieved by a lot of other people. The problem is they "could not find a way" to take the first steps to achieve their success. They hesitated to get started, "could not" find a way to save money, nor develop the first draft of a business plan. For them their pain and frustrations were real, however their fear prevented them from achieving success, their fear was in their mind.

Often, the steps are simple, easy and obvious. The key is to get started, take action, observe your results, adjust accordingly, and take more action. Most of the actions people take when they set out to achieve a goal are "Wrong". We learn by trial and error. When we try anything for the first time, we are bound to make mistakes. but mistakes are not failures! They are simply the best, smartest action we could figure out at the time, but unfortunately they may not give us the results we desire, so we learn and try again. Did you fall down when you first tried to walk? Probably, were your first attempts at dating clumsy or embarrassing? Probably. Were your first attempts to use a computer frustrating? Probably. There is no failure or shame in trying. We try, we learn, and we try again. The key to getting anything you want in life is to take action. Take the smartest, best action you can think of and see what happens. If you can, hire a mentor or coach to help you. But take some action. Observe your results, adjust accordingly, and keep on keeping on.

Famous Quotes

"In any moment of decision, the best thing you can do is the right thing. The worst thing you can do is nothing."
Theodore Roosevelt

"Most of the things worth doing in the world have been declared impossible before they were attempted."
Earl Nightingale

The 5 Great Reiki Principles

Just for Today I will let go of Anger.
Just for Today I will let go of Worry.
Just for Today I will give thanks for my many blessings.
Just for Today I will do my work honestly.
Just for Today I will be kind to my neighbor and every living being. Author Anon

Maya Angelou said:
"I've learned that no matter what happens, or how bad it seems today, life does go on, and it will be better tomorrow."
"I've learned that you can tell a lot about a person by the way he/she handles these three things: a rainy day, lost luggage, and tangled Christmas tree lights."
"I've learned that regardless of your relationship with your parents, you'll miss them when they're gone from your life."
"I've learned that making a "living" is not the same thing as "making a life.""
"I've learned that life sometimes gives you a second chance."
"I've learned that you shouldn't go through life with a catcher's mitt on both hands; you need to be able to throw some things back."
"I've learned that whenever I decide something with an open heart, I usually make the right decision."
"I've learned that even when I have pains; I don't have to be one."
"I've learned that every day you should reach out and touch someone.
People love a warm hug or just a friendly pat on the back."
"I've learned that I still have a lot to learn."
"I've learned that people will forget what you said, people

will forget what you did, but people will never forget how you made them feel."
                Maya Angelou

15 Steps to Strengthening Your Coping Skills

Here are some steps you can take to build up resilience, strengthen your coping skills, and make adversity work for you: 1. Practice failing. Look for opportunities to put yourself in difficult situations where you might fall flat on your face. Resiliency develops when we acknowledge our weaknesses and flaws. If you are in an environment where nothing challenging happens, you won't have the motivation to learn how to bounce back.

2. Take small risks. Don't allow the fear of failure to keep you from trying something new. Seek out challenges and look for new ways of doing things. When you bounce back from the small catastrophes, you will be strengthening the coping skills to rebound from the big ones.

3. Shake off the victim stance. Give yourself a set amount of time to feel sorry for yourself or grieve a loss, then move on. When you are invited to a "poor me" personal pity-party, you can agree to show up, but don't stay long. Instead of moaning, "What a loser I am!" or, "Everything happens to me," tell yourself that just because you have a failure now doesn't mean you are a failure. Don't take it personally and refuse to let it define who you are.

4. Check your explanatory style. The way you explain problems, hitches, complications, and the world around you affects your adaptability. Optimists have the ability to attribute difficulties to transitory, nonpermanent conditions rather than to personal inadequacies, enduring weaknesses,

or inherent flaws. They recognize that everything is temporary and nothing is permanent. To them, it was simply a demanding customer or a computer glitch or a bad-hair day. Pessimists, on the other hand, think it's a lasting condition and assume personal responsibility for every failure. Even when they achieve success, they see it as sheer luck, a fluke, or a coincidence.

5. Regain your perspective. You'll have a better chance at bouncing back if you can step away from the situation and get a view of the bigger picture. Detach yourself and ask what this will mean to you in five or ten years. Positive reframing will give you a fresh perspective with which to evaluate what has happened to you and decide whether it is worth losing inner peace over it.

6. Become flexible. Do you remember Gumby, the little animated green-clay character? You may have watched his adventures with Pokey and the gang on television. Well, the thing about Gumby is that he is so bendable and pliable. This little guy is as supple as you can get. He can be stretched all out of shape and then spring right back into form again. Does that sound like you? If you don't have some flexibility or know how to give a little when you're stretched, you will eventually break in two. Being rigid causes you to crack when difficulties and hardships strike.

7. Quit recycling old emotions. You can easily get caught in the rut of developing one long, drawn-out excuse for why you still have problems years later. We could all find a reason to be the way we are; none of us has a valid reason to stay that way.

8. Make the best of the worst. People who bounce back from past setbacks and move confidently into the future believe that whatever the problem, they will make

something good come from it. At a large corporation where I presented one of my workshops, employees Deanna and Shelly were both notified that their company was downsizing. They knew they would lose their jobs. Shelley's first thought was, "This is the worst thing that could ever happen to me. I can't see myself ever pulling through." Deanna, although initially devastated, eventually came to the place where she thought, I've always wondered what it would be like to turn my hobby into a business. Now it looks like I'm going to have the chance! Decide to first assess the new reality and then look for innovative ways to adapt.

9. Learn to curb emotions and keep them in check. Most of us react emotionally to a major crisis, or even a minor setback. Feelings of anger, sadness, anxiety, or fear are appropriate and normal. But people who recover from misfortune don't wallow in those emotions. In the face of conflict or crisis, resilient people exercise self-control. They don't ride out feelings of intense anger and anxiety. They also don't lash out and burn bridges; rather, they maintain relationships and keep doors open. Women who focus too much on their feelings about a situation do not cope well with life's challenges.

10. Develop a flexible thinking style. Being able to recognize the opportunities within a setback takes a special kind of open-mindedness. All of us have a unique thinking style, our own way of processing the information that shapes and defines our perceptions. The problem is that our perceptions, especially in the midst of adversity, are often inaccurate. Whether true or false, our thoughts and perceptions drive our emotions and behaviors. Practice getting out of your habitual way of thinking and be flexible when you look at problems.

11. Choose to be positive. People who consistently make the best out of difficult circumstances tend to be optimistic. No matter how bad things get, they are usually able to say, "Bad things aren't going to be bad forever." Rigid people tend to believe things will never change. Survivors imagine possibilities that are not anywhere in sight right now. They can envision a way out of a dead-end job or an abusive relationship. They tend to believe, "If anyone can do it, why not me?"

12. Find the humor. A sense of humor is a wonderful coping device and a main ingredient in resiliency. Seeing things from a funny standpoint helps you have some emotional distance and view the situation from a new perspective. Lighten up and have a good laugh at yourself while you're at it. (By the way, if you haven't laughed at yourself lately, somebody else probably has!) People who can laugh at themselves and their mistakes will never cease to be amused! You'll be healthier for it, too. As the Bible says, A merry heart doeth good like a medicine (Proverbs 17:22 KJV).

13. Build a strong support network. Be brave enough to seek help and encouragement from others. Although I always felt that self-sufficiency went hand in hand with being resilient, it wasn't until I began reaching out to others for positive support that I gained the strength to recover and the courage to make constructive changes. Look for family members, friends, other survivors, or a support group where people are trustworthy, available, and willing to rally round you in your darkest hours. They can pray for you and with you, coach you through your experience. Your support group can also be thee to celebrate in your recovery. An old Irish proverb states, "It is in the shelter of each other that people live."

14. Rely on faith, not fate. Trust in God to bring you through. Your life is in His hands and is not dependent on fate, chance, or coincidences. When you believe in fate, you are trusting outside circumstances and external influences. Instead, believe in "divine intervention" and watch for miracles to happen. My own personal transformation happened when I first became aware that you and I are not human beings trying to discover our spirituality, but rather we are spiritual beings having a human experience here on earth. Life's challenges have a way of bringing us face-to-face with our Creator and the realization that there is a divine plan for our lives: The God of all grace, who called you to his eternal glory in Christ, after you have suffered a little while, will himself restore you and make you strong, firm and steadfast (1 Peter 5:10).

15. Be a giver. Get involved in a worthy cause. The Bible says, "Let us not love with words or tongue but with actions and in truth" (1 John 3:18). See where you can volunteer your time, talents and energy. Sue Augustine Resiliency comes with finding ways to make a valuable contribution. The more you get connected to the bigger things in life, beyond yourself, the more pliable you will be. Being involved with your church, community, or a larger cause helps put your personal problems into perspective. People who live self-absorbed, "me-centered" lives have greater difficulty finding meaning in their life and don't weather trauma as well. As Lucy Lucom said, "If the world seems cold to you, kindle fires to warm it."

Success Is a Personal Journey
A Glance Back Toward the Starting Line

Through out the years I've realized that life can be unpredictable and a person can never really know what hurdle will fall into his/hers path. From disappointing athletic performances to overwhelming health crises, I've definitely had my fair share of obstacles to overcome. But there is one thing I've learned during these challenging times, you can never give up or get down on yourself. A true champion keeps his or her chin up and always takes life one race at a time. This is how I keep focused on my goals and racing toward my dreams.

Finding my stride
I was born on Nov. 19, 1966 in Seattle, Washington. My family later moved to National City California, a small town in San Diego, County. Although I was born in the Pacific Northwest, Southern California is where I call "home". Since I was a young girl, I've always been a runner. In fact my brother Parenthesis (PD) used to race me and then tease me when I lost. Well one day, I decided I was just not going to lose anymore. So I started practicing, and it paid off. I beat PD the next time we raced, and he never raced me again. From then on, running was all that mattered. I had found my stride.
I ran all through high school and was heavily recruited by major universities. I chose the University of California at Los Angeles and joined UCLA's track team where the 100-meter hurdles became my top events. In fact I set an American record in 100-meter hurdles during my senior year in 1988. And I've continued to break my record -- most recently on July 23, 2000. In addition to my track and field success, I also enjoyed academic success at UCLA, earning a bachelor's degree in sociology.

Beating the odds

Despite my athletic success, 1988 was also the year I encountered one of the toughest challenges of my life. While training for the Olympics in Seoul, South Korea, my health began to deteriorate. I suffered migraine headaches, sleeplessness, fainting spells and frequent vision loss. I should have been at my peak performance. Instead, I was constantly exhausted and my body felt out of control.

At first I blamed my condition on the pressures of Olympic training. But I soon found out that I had Graves' disease, a debilitating chronic thyroid disorder. During this time my feet became so blistered and swollen, the skin cracked and bled. The excruciating pain forced me to stop running. The doctors were sure they would have to amputate both of my feet. I was devastated. Deep down, I was scared to death that my life as an athlete was over. But I wasn't going to give up; the word "quit" has never been the part of my vocabulary. With lots of hard work, determination, perseverance and faith in God, I was able to resume training and regain my health. In 1992, less than 17 months after the doctors had considered amputating my feet, I won my first gold medal in 100-meter dash at the Olympics in Barcelona, Spain, and was named the "World's Fastest Woman." I knew I was `back!

Crossing the finish line

During 1993, I continued my winning streak, earning seven championship tittles. At the world championships at Stuttgart, Germany, I accomplished a feat that hadn't been achieved in 45 years; I won both the 100-meter dash and 100-meter hurdles. Then in 1995, I secured the No.1 U.S. ranking for the 100-meter hurdles after winning the National Champion and World Champion tittles.

During the 1996 Olympic Games in Atlanta, I repeated my 1992 performance by winning the gold medal in 100-meter dash, becoming only the second woman to win the prestigious event at two consecutive Olympics. I was also on the gold medal-winning 4x100 meter relay team. Gail Devers

Chapter 6

The Sex Revolution

We have always been a sexual people. In Pensacola Florida, where I grew up, Black boys said they would not wear a "rubber" (condom) when having sexual intercourse. They said "they did not want to put a rain coat on; they wanted to feel the real thing". And as you can guess there were plenty of babies being born and a lot of gonorrhea and syphilis spread through sexual contact. My goal was to graduate from high school without being pregnant. I knew that the only way for that to happen was for me to be a virgin or be an old maid. My aunt in Chicago was a nurse and I was determined to become a nurse like her. It was customary then that if a boy got a girl pregnant, the father of the girl visited the boy and he had to marry her.

As a young girl, I saw the lady across the street from our house (called fish bone, because she was tall and thin) have one man after another come into her house for sex (prostitution). No one in the community said anything about it. Also, living in the next block was a "sissy" (now, who is called a male homosexual), both were accepted. None of the adults or the ministers said anything. In fact, due to segregation, in my neighborhood, we had teachers, preachers, wino's (alcoholics), insurance men, people with nice homes and cars all living together. We did not have any thieves, everyone knew everyone who entered your home, and everyone watched everyone's house and questioned strangers in the neighborhood. Strangers had to give their name, address, and tell who they were looking for and why.

Everyone was "nosey" and into everyone's business. There were no secrets. Whenever my father visited a woman's house, even in another part of the city, my mom was notified. We did not have a telephone. We were too poor to own a telephone. My cousins across the street from us had a phone. The biggest "sin" or thing most young people did to get in trouble was smoke cigarettes, and drink alcohol. However, there was a big emphasis on getting an education to advance the Black race. We wanted to prove to white people that we were intelligent and could act "civilized" (act, speak and dress proper).

Today our sexual habits and patterns are wiping out our race. Are you concerned, do you care? What do you feel could help persons of the age 40 and under? In the olden days, a boy would ask the father if he could date the girl and he took responsibility to marry the girl if she became pregnant. Then our sexual behavior was a community affair. Today people have sexual affairs and think no one knows or see them. Your sexual habits, practices and preference is a personal matter, however what is done in the dark, my mom used to say "will come to the light."

Sometimes, only God and the Angels know our dirty secrets. The secret behaviors, we do in the dark will come to the light often in the form of a sexually transmitted disease. Today, bisexuality, (men having sexual intercourse with both women and men) "down low" sex activity, is on the increase. There is an increasing number of women (lesbian) and homosexual male relationships. Are we a failure when it comes to healthy heterosexual relationships? There also is the tendency of Black men to have multiple sex partners. Infidelity is on the increase. Some black men are homophobic, non committal to a relationship with a Black woman or have negative ideas regarding tender feelings like love. It is difficult to see a black man pushing a Black baby in a stroller, yet they are rushing to produce mixed race babies, that they are proud to hold and show in public. Many Black men will have sex with and get a black girl pregnant, but marry a white, Mexican or Asian girl. Where is the pride in your black skin and black race? These are issues we must face in the Black community if our race is to survive.

Down Low's, the Silent Killers

We used to have rules for dating, relating and having sex. Today, Black men are whispering a lot of sweet words in the ear of Black women while they have sex with other men. Let's have sex responsibly and with integrity. If a man chooses to have sex with a man, he should remain with men and leave women alone. A man cannot say he loves Black women, and have sex with both a woman and a man. Black men love and respect yourself enough to do the right thing, buy and wear a condom, if you choose to have sex. When you love someone you act responsibly before engaging in sex. You make sure you take the necessary precautions to buy and use a condom to prevent the transmission of a sexually transmitted disease.

What do you think is behind the insanity of having sexual intercourse without using a condom protection? I believe it is lack of respect for the life and welfare of Black women and lack of respect and appreciation for the Black race? When you think about it the, only people who would have unprotected sex in 2006 is someone suicidal or desperate for sex. We cannot live without oxygen, but we can live without sex. There is a misconception about love and relationship that we have to accept anything and anyone. We can choose to wait until God sends us the right partner. Rushing to have sex with the wrong person will kill you, waiting to find the right person, while you develop your self and your skills will prolong your life, enhance your self-esteem and put money in your pockets to invest or buy your first home. Let us set an example for our young black boys by encouraging them to pull up their sagging pants, pick up a book to read and strive to graduate from college.

    I am aware there are three girl babies born for every male child. There is an over abundance of women, however I do not believe we need to share men. I propose a new concept of shared friendship without sex.
The men who remain single can have friendships with some women and have only one sexual relationship. The women would have to agree to the contract with their signature and make sure they do not break the contract by becoming sexually involved with the male if he is in a committed sex partner/relationship. The women could agree to spend one or two week ends with the man with the majority of the time with his primary relationship. I know the trend today is to live together and never get married. I am against that life style, especially if there are children involved. Both girls and especially boys need to see other men taking care of a family.

    Today, the trend is for people to live together and never marry. This creates single parent homes. All children need to see and be part of a two parent family of which I was fortunate to experience. Even though my dad and mom drank alcohol on the weekend, they gave us a stable home environment Monday through Friday. My dad never stayed a night away from our home even on the weekends he insisted that my mom be home before 2 am when she went out to party. Another behavior that was practiced in the South (Pensacola, Florida), is that the mother and father did not both go out of the house at night to party until the oldest child was twelve years old. Twelve was the magic number for a girl to start taking over house hold duties. I did not like the age twelve arrangement. It was too much responsibility for me. I had to give up my childhood and grow up faster than I wanted. I did not like taking care of my younger brother and sister. I was often mean to them; to this day they still talk about it. However, I have to remind them that I was a child also and not ready to give up my play time to take care of them.

Back then, many girls experimented with sexual intercourse and many became pregnant like my older sister. My sister had a strong sex drive and I was like an ice cube. Sex did not interest me because my goal was set on becoming a nurse like my aunt Ida who lived in Chicago. After graduation from high school, I started making plans to move to Chicago. Enrolling in Provident Hospital, the Black co-ed school of nursing. The hospital where Dr. Daniel Hale Williams performed the first open heart surgery.

Chapter 7

AIDS, What You Don't Know, Can Kill You

AIDS is a great plague upon all humanity that has already claimed the lives of more than 23 million men, women and children worldwide. With an estimated 38 million people throughout the globe currently living with HIV all current predictions tell us that this is just the beginning of this epidemic.
The American International AIDS Foundation, publisher of AIDS.com, believes that their mission of "Sharing Hope and Providing Knowledge" will promote better awareness of this disease and its prevention.

Here are some of the alarming facts of this tragedy:
3.1 million People lost their lives in 2005.
4.9 million People were newly infected with HIV in 2005.
40.3 million People around the world are living with AIDS/HIV in 2005.
Approximately 11 of every 1,000 adults (ages 15 to 49) are HIV infected.
25 million children will be orphans by 2010 because of AIDS.
Over 27 million people have died since the first AIDS case was identified in 1980.

AIDS and HIV do not discriminate. It is devastating to people of all ages, genders, races, religions and nationalities irregardless if you're gay, straight, a drug user or not. It can reach you in the most innocent of ways and that is what makes AIDS so dangerous. While there is no cure at this time (only treatment) for the AIDS virus, it can be prevented through education, awareness and precautionary methods, including HIV home testing kits offered through www.aids.com.

NPR Commentary States, The Black Community Should Discuss Behavioral Factors Involved in HIV Transmission, and Target Black Men. HIV/AIDS "remains an unspoken taboo among Blacks, in the United States, despite the grim health statistics of a high number of Black Americans dying of AIDS. Amy Alexander, an author and media critic, said in a commentary on NPR's "News & Notes with Ed Gordon" that Black officials, clergy and community activists are not discussing the behavioral factors involved in HIV transmission in a manner that is helpful, rational, and likely to educate Black Americans about the high stakes involved because of the "combination of lack of funding, political will, shame and stigma" Alexander says, because Black men are historically averse to seeking medical care, especially for mental or emotional issues, those struggling with drug addiction or questioning their sexual identity would rather suffer in silence than seek the help of clinical professionals.

Black men, who engage in behaviors that put them at risk of contracting HIV, continue to carry on unattended, untouched by the public service messages and the educational campaigns designed to reinforce healthy behavior. The denial, shame and stigma that continue to surround Blacks and HIV must be stopped before the Black community is extinguished.

There are many myths surrounding the origin of AIDS. It was rumored that it was first started when a white man had sex with a monkey; In addition, it was thought that whites brought the disease to Africa. None of these theories have been proven to be true, however the important belief that the disease started and was confined to Africa, may have led many African Americans to believe that it would not affect them, since they had no intention of going to Africa. What we as American Africans, failed to realize was that the HIV virus which causes AIDS is transmitted through the blood stream. This means that where ever blood exists on our body and the skin is broken, the virus can enter the body. The most common routes of skin breakage are during sexual intercourse, and through direct puncture of the skin with a needle to inject methamphetamine, cocaine and crystal methamphetamine, through blood vein of the body. Both of these routes of the transmission of the HIV virus, which causes AIDS, can be prevented.

If you had sexual intercourse with only one partner, the disease could not spread; or if the man used a condom each time he had sex with another partner, the disease could not spread. The problem is young black male's state that they did not want to wear a condom, put a "raincoat" over their penis because "they can not feel the real thing". Our desire to "feel the real thing" is both irresponsible and suicidal, on the part of both women and men. I understand that our youth is the largest population to get infected today due to unprotected sex. This is unfortunate; most youth think they are invincible. Maybe many Black men are slow to grow up and the women who have sexual intercourse with them are desperate for sex or to have a man in their presence. All of this is the mindset of a mentally unstable person. We had better wake up, and start talking about this matter, before the black race is wiped out. I suggest we start having small focus groups, AIDS discussion groups in the church, in the beauty shops and definitely at the dinner tables in our homes.

Chapter 8

The Sellout of Jesus and the Black Church

The church and the Black community have allowed Jesus to become big business in Hollywood and many of the Mega churches. All of the major Black movies use the church as a tool to attract women to attend the theatre to boost their box office sales. Jesus is no longer, the one who saves our soul. He can be bought for a few dollars to make you feel good. And getting the Holy Spirit on television churches and in the movies seems to be a game of who has the best showmanship skills. The last time I read my Bible, it said salvation was free and that we could go to God and Jesus anytime we wanted. We do not need a special Bible or a special person to pray for us or to anoint us.

I agree that church fellowship is wonderful; however some male Ministers prey on our love for Jesus and our emotions as women to our disadvantage. Jesus is free to all who seek Him: The wino, prostitute, gambler and homeless. I wonder sometimes if this is what has caused some people to stray from the church, fearing they are not "holy enough" and that people seem insincere about their relationship with Jesus, or some people may feel that they are a "sinner". God love sinners, because they realize they need His help. A well person does not need a doctor; likewise someone who is saved may not feel the need to ask forgiveness for their sins or believe they can daily do things that are not pleasing in God's sight and feel no need to change their ways. We do not need to buy Jesus, the Holy Spirit or God. All of this has been freely given to us. Some people seem to have a light hearted and casual feeling about themselves, their relationships, God and the church. It is hard to know who or what is real. When I was growing up in the 50's, people seemed genuine in their communication, they seemed to care about how you felt and life had more meaning than it does today. Today everything and everyone seems to be on a fast moving roller coaster existence. Grandmothers were someone who took you to church and made teacakes. Like my grandmother who grew a garden with corn, collard greens, snap green beans, watermelons and grapes.

Today, a grandmother has a new role. In the movie, "Diary of a Mad Black woman" Madea does not believe in going to church or reading the bible. The bible is shown in several scenes, however, the wisdom of the Bible and grandmothers is lost, and so are the moral values. Madea curses throughout the movie. The elderly uncle corrupts young adults and children by smoking marijuana in front of them. The only saving grace of the movies is that the abusive husband and drug dealing wife find their way to ask forgiveness and join the church. This is not the only movie that exploits the church. Jesus and the Black community are being exploited by Black movie makers and rap artists. The young Black entertainers who travel abroad give the impression that we are a culture of people with no refinement, class or intelligence. This is a sad misrepresentation of African Americans

The Church and the minister have shifted from being a part of the family. We used to have Sunday dinner with our pastor and his family. It seems a lot of the focus is on getting more people into the Church, to get more money. I realize Churches need to pay their obligations, and I support that. There are financial expenses in running a church that cripple small churches, however in a smaller church you get the feeling of being part of a family that you lose in a huge mega church. Many of the larger churches are into mass psychology and mass marketing. For example the church sermon "Woman Thou Art Loose" by

TD Jakes has been turned into a CD and soon will a movie. Religion and Jesus is being sold to make people feel good. I am not saying that loving Jesus should make us feel bad. It is just that our love for Jesus can be used by some people to manipulate and control us. Both God and Jesus' love for you is free and you can talk to both in your heart anytime day or night. We Black people love having a sense of community and some churches gives us this. I don't think the old fashioned minister exist any more, who comes by your house to visit. However, I know a fabulous minister, Reverend Clarice Christian in San Diego, who is anointed, filled with the holy spirit, has great healing hands, and to whom you can call for free and talk about any problem. Reverend Christian is doing what the old fashioned male ministers used to do.

Our world is very complex today; we are separated from our families, and often live alone in a city of stranger. I suggest you take the time to develop a personal relationship with Jesus, so that you can call Him when you can't find a minister to help reinforce the power of your prayers. It seems God is calling women into the ministry to preach every day. Many of our single and married male ministers have allowed their feelings and emotions for women in the church to get them side tracked from their mission. However, we cannot despair because God said we would be tempted and surely that is the case today. I feel that as Black people we have lost our moral compass. We used to be able to talk about the evil and sins of other races of people now we have little room to criticize anyone. Black people are doing any and everything. I am certain God is heart broken over how we have lost our way. One comforting note is that there are still some Black folks on bended knees and they are to be commended for staying the course. We need you and more like you. Continue to pray for our children, the Black family, our Black boys and our

Black men, who have abandoned Black women and the Black race for greener pastures. Our Black families are falling apart with women as head of households, and no male role models for our Black boys except what they see on television.

Our nuclear family is rapidly disappearing; however our church family connections are becoming weaker because we live so far apart from each other. One new trend that is happening at my church is the church newsletter and e-mail; it is a way to know what is happening in the church community. It is especially helpful when someone dies during the week so you can call or send a condolence card to the family.

One trend I have noticed in churches is that no one corrects our youth on what is appropriate and inappropriate dress ware. Many of the young girls' clothing are so tight, you can see the imprint of their under ware, and their breast exposure is enough to excite and stimulate any male whether he has a cloak or is a fellow pew member.
Many children and adults chew gum in church; the children do not address the elders with a title such as Mrs. or Ms. Everything is oriented toward the youth, so we do not have our distinction of elders who can advise or spiritually mentor our youth. Many youth do not respect their elders and will curse and use foul language in their presence.

We have certainly lost the A-men corner where the elders used to sit and pray. I suggest we grab hold of the new, as we hold on to our old time religious values. There has to be a deliberate effort to single out those persons who want to be acknowledged as an Elder in the Church and make an appropriate mention of them each Sunday at Church.

It would help if we sang some of the old spiritual and hymnals to get us in a prayerful mood and spirit. There are so many things that compete for our attention. I would love to have each member assigned to a prayer partner each year which they would exchange the first Sunday in each New Year.

All I Need To Know About Life I Learned From My Guardian Angel

Know all the possibilities of your impossible dream
Leave space in your relationships so you'll have lots of room to play.
Be yourself. Forgive, forget and forge ahead.
It's easier to fly when you take yourself lightly.
Reach out and touch someone lightly with your wing.
Love is the only four letter word you need to know.
Whenever you hear a bell, another angel
 has earned their wings.
It's okay to cry during sad movies.
Don't postpone joy to scrub the bathroom
 or clean the garage.
Love mother earth... Whenever you feel afraid, get a new box of crayons.
Carry a spare set of wings in your pocket.
Wherever you go, that is where you will be.
Spread your wings and fly.
      Author Unknown

Chapter 9

Domestic Violence, Emotional Abuse, It's Affect on the Family

There are many stressors on the Black family today. Violence and abuse affect the lives of everyone. Often the strain of lack of employment for the Black man, lack of respect, limited financial resources, and the pressures of being a Black man in society creates a ticking time bond waiting to explode. Often the Black man cannot put into words his frustrations about feeling insignificant, humiliation and lack of control over his outer world. He is often the victim of racial profiling and discrimination. The Black man is feared he will rob or kill people. He is watched and his every move is critiqued. When he walks by, people grab their purses. All of these events along with the pressures of miscommunication in a normal relationship often erupt in a verbal or physical altercation with his intimate partner or wife, and it is labeled domestic violence.

Domestic violence is a physical altercation in an intimate relationship where one or both parties are at risk to be injured. Usually there is an underlying element of power and control that leads to one of the parties trying to over power the other. Often it is the male who engages in shoving, pushing, punching, arguing, shouting, yelling, threatening and intimidation of his female partner which results in a call to the police to resolve the conflict. The situation on occasion can be threatening if one of the parties uses a knife or gun to resolve the dispute. Often these arguments occur in the presence of children, who are frightened and traumatized with fear that the mother will be killed by her husband or male companion. In some case children or a neighbor will call the police to stop the violence for fear someone will get hurt. It is sad and scary when two adults are unable to resolve their conflict without resorting to violence. When I was a teenager my mom and dad got into a pushing, shoving argument and my brother started fighting my dad. It alarmed both my brother and dad; however it made him rethink before he attempted to touch my mom again. Because as a child I witnessed that abuse. I married a man who physically abused me, whom I divorced and put in jail. We become the product of what we see, hear and experience.

In California, where I live, whenever the police are called for domestic violence, one and sometime both parties will go to jail. If the woman scratches or injures the male, she will go to jail, have to take a 52 week domestic violence training while her children are placed in a foster home. If the mother continues to have a relationship or communicate with the offender of the violence (perpetrator) she could lose custody of her children. Situations of this nature could benefit from conflict resolution or anger management training skills for both parties. If both parties worked on self management and self control, domestic violence could be prevented. Until couples find a way to resolve their disputes, domestic violence or intimidate partner abuse will continue to tear relationships and families apart. If any of the practices mentioned in the following paragraphs were implemented before an argument, domestic violence and intimidate partner abuse could be eradicated. We coach by phone on these issues at www.selfesteemcenter.org or (619) 262-9951.

The Effects of Anger on Your Relationships

Your anger is not caused by events in the world but by you and your private thoughts. What I mean by this is the things you tell yourself in your mind are what cause your reactions mentally and physically. If your perception of a situation is distorted, then so will be your thoughts and feelings about the situation. If you tell yourself that you are offended, scared, and fearful then you will believe this and take on those characteristics. Your responses at this time are a choice: To cover up your feelings and project a false front, or to own your feelings and work through them. You need to recognize that you should talk back to your private thoughts more and question them. You can take a "cooling off" period and gather your composure, or you can re-examine the situation and do problem-solving. If you are fearful then you need to explore what you think is causing your fear. If it is a feeling of inadequacy, you need to ask yourself why you feel inadequate. If it is a feeling of being personally attacked then you need to ask yourself, if this is really happening and why you feel so vulnerable and threatened

Improvement in your communication skills can be a plus, because it would help you to be clearer in your speaking or explaining your feelings without being rushed, angry or feeling intimidated. You create your anger by giving in to your private thoughts of perceived abuse. Doing things that will increase your self esteem and get rid of feelings of worthlessness, will help all parties involved.

Distract Yourself to Control Your Anger
Our mind has difficulty focusing on two subjects at once. When we start thinking about something new, we stop thinking about what is making us angry. By distracting

our attention away from what aggravates us we can short circuit our anger.

The ABC's of Distracting Yourself
A. After deciding that there is no effective way to change anger arousing situation, choose to distract yourself.
B. Take a "time out" from the situation by devoting your attention to some less annoying focus such as a magazine, a radio program, people watching, or fantasy.
C. If you succeed, reward yourself with a mental pat on the back. If a distraction doesn't work, try another strategy like walking.

Avoid Over Stimulation
Hostile people are often in a highly agitated state. This state may be heightened by nicotine, caffeine, sweets, drugs or alcohol. Using less of these substances can help reduce your anger.

The ABC's to Avoid Over Stimulation
A. Make it a goal to cut back as much as you can or eliminate nicotine, caffeine, sweets, alcohol, and drugs.
B. Set a goal to exercise several times a week.
C. Congratulate yourself when you achieve your goals; accept that it is common to fail, and simply begin anew.

Anger is triggered by external events called provocations. Provocations create anger thoughts, anger arousal and anger actions, which all escalate each other until they are fused together like three prongs on a pitchfork in an anger feedback loop that leads to destructive consequences.

HOW TO MANAGE YOUR ANGER

1. Anger does not have to be released like steam in a pressure cooker.
2. Venting/Expressing your anger makes you feel better only for a moment, and then regret, disappointment and sorrow follow an emotional outburst.
3. The first step is to figure out what is causing you to get angry or react in an angry way.
4. What Are You Saying to Yourself Inside Your Head?
5. Do you feel victimized, taken advantage of, disrespected, ignored, not acknowledged?
6. Do you have a fear of rejection?
7. Do you like yourself? People who like themselves do not need to prove to someone they are right.
8. People who like themselves do not take or interpret things others say to them as a personal offense. They can give the other person the benefit of the doubt or let things pass without responding.

Anger the Emotion (Conflict, Criticism or Anger)
The Activating Event is Something That Happens, a Stimulus or Trigger. It is:
   A. Belief system you have about the activating event. Do I believe this is a good thing?
   B. A consequence of the belief of our emotional response, examples happiness. The key to happiness is to change our belief system.
   C. Realize life is difficult and conflict is normal. Life is lessons to be lessons to be learned.
   D. You are responsible for your life situation and responses.
   E. You must manage your expectations of people, situations and yourself.

F. Work on the gap between your <u>expectations</u> and <u>what you are</u> receiving<u>.</u> Work on managing yourself.
G. Identify where you are now and where you want to go.
H. Decide what is important and develop a plan of action.
I. Avoid responding to the activating event of others.

ANGER RESOLUTION

Anger is a valuable signal; it lets you know when something is wrong and need to be corrected. The critical factor is whether your expression of anger is adding to your problem or solving your problem. **Often when we are angry one of these things are going on:**

1. We want something and we are not getting it.
2. From past experience, we expect trouble.
3. We feel powerless to get what we want.

The premise of anger management techniques is for you to use your anger as a signal to identify your problem and deal with it: Rather that act upon your anger by lashing out, to make the situation worse or to hold your angry feelings inside.

1. **Anger can lead to:** 1. Angrily lashing out → to make the situation worse
2. Hold feelings inside → creates resentment, physical symptoms

Or

You can identify the problem to handle or solve it. You do this by changing the thoughts you think. This is helpful when thinking about something that irritates you or makes you mad.

When a situation provokes you and you are preparing to respond, begin thinking and ask yourself some critical questions:
1. How can I manage this situation?
2. What is it that I absolutely have to do?
3. Decide how you will regulate your anger?
4. Will an argument between you and the other person solve your problem?
5. Do you have a plan, for time to calm down or relax when angry?

Alternatives to Angrily Acting Out
Rethink, To Change Your Expression of Anger, You Must Change Your Thinking
Change what you say to yourself in your head, in response to the external event.
Take time to **rethink** about what has provoked you.
1. Use a planned relaxation technique
2. Stay calm and keep your cool
3. Ask yourself if you are overreacting, taking things too seriously, or justifying your right to be angry.

How to Cool Down When You Are Angry

1. Use an anger mantra like:
   "I am in control of my anger"
   "I choose not to get angry"
   "It is not ok for me to blow up/get angry/ act crazy/lose it"

2. **Recognize your triggers or hot buttons**
   What makes/causes you to get angry? **Keep an anger calendar** whenever you allow yourself to fly into rage, mark the date with an "x" on your calendar to see how often this happens.

3. **Avoid name calling, accusing, blaming judging, belittling** or any put downs to elevate your self esteem.

4. **Deal with the real issue**
   - Are you overreacting?
   - Are you addicted to conflict for excitement to engage the attention of someone?
   - Do you get angry to have others notice you?
   - Are you desperate for attention, even negative kind, and will do anything to get it?

Assertiveness Inventory to Avoid Conflict and Create More Intimacy

The following question will be helpful in assessing our assertiveness. Be honest in your responses. All you have to do is draw circle around the number that describes you best. For some questions the assertive end of the scale is at 0, for others at 4. Key: 0 means no or never; 1 means somewhat or sometimes; 2 means average; 3 means usually or a good deal; and 4 means practically always or entirely.

1. When a person is highly unfair, do you call it to his attention?..0 1 2 3 4
2. Do you find it difficult to make decision...0 1 2 3 4
3. Are you openly critical of others' ideas, opinions, behavior?...0 1 2 3 4
4. Do you speak out in protest when someone takes your place in line?..0 1 2 3 4
5. Do you often avoid people or situations for fear of embarrassment 0 1 2 3 4
6. Do you usually have confidence in your own judgment?..0 1 2 3 4
7. Do you insist that your spouse/roommate take a fair share of household chores?........................0.1 2 3 4
8. Are you prone to "fly off the handle" 0 1 2 3 4

9. When a salesman makes an effort do you find it hard to say "No" even though the merchandise is not really what you want? 0 1 2 3 4
10. When a latecomer is waited on before you are, do you call attention to the situation? 0 1 2 3 4
11. Are you reluctant to speak up in a discussion or debate? 0 1 2 3 4
12. If a person has borrowed money (a book, garment, thing of value) and is overdue in returning it, do you mention it? 0 1 2 3 4
13. Do you continue to pursue an argument after the other person has finished?...........................0 1 2 3 4
14. Do you generally express what you feel? ..0 1 2 3 4
15. Are you disturbed if someone watches you at work? 0 1 2 3 4
16. If someone keeps kicking or bumping your chair in a movie or a lecture, do you ask the person to stop? 0 1 2 3 4
17. Do you find it difficult to keep eye contact when talking to another person?............................0 1 2 3 4
18. In a good restaurant, when your meal is improperly prepared or served, do you ask a waiter/waitress to correct the situation?...................................0 1 2 3 4
19. When you discover merchandise is faulty, do you return it for an adjustment?..........................0 1 2 3 4
20. Do you show your anger by name-calling or obscenities?..0 1 2 3 4
21. Do you try to be a wallflower or a piece of the furniture in social situations?......................0 1 2 3 4
22. Do you insist that your landlord (mechanic, repairman) make repairs, adjustments or replacements which are his responsibility?0 1 2 3 4
23. Do you often step in and make decisions for others? 0 1 2 3 4
24. Are you able openly to express love and affection? 0 1 2 3 4

25. Are you able to ask your friends for small favors or help?...0 1 2 3 4
26. Do you think you always have the right answer? 0 1 2 3 4
27. When you differ with a person you respect, are you able to speak up for yourself or viewpoint? 0 1 2 3 4
28. Are you able to refuse unreasonable requests made by friends?..0 1 2 3 4
29. Do you have difficulty complimenting or praising others?..0 1 2 3 4
30. If disturbed by someone smoking near you, do you say so?..0 1 2 3 4

Healthy Relationship Communication

There are some specific skills that you can learn to use to improve communication with another person. The optimal way to improve communication in a relationship is for both partners to learn and practice the skills together. But even if your partner doesn't happen to be learning with you, one person using these skills can have an impact on a relationship.

This approach to communication is based upon the following three assumptions. The first basic assumption is that feelings, all kinds, EXIST. They are neither good nor bad, wrong or right, correct or incorrect, they just ARE. The second assumption is that all of us have the right to have any feeling in the world. Some behaviors or actions may need to be limited, but any feeling is okay. And each one of us is the ultimate authority on our own feelings. No <u>one</u> can tell you what you do or do not feel. Another person may not like what you are feeling or may feel differently. But no one can tell you that you do not feel the way you do.

The third assumption is that an intimate relationship, at its best, is a place where both partners feel safe to share feeling, when they choose to, without getting attacked for doing so.

Ineffective Coping Skills, Communication Patterns to Avoid For Healthy Relationships

The Summarizing Self Syndrome
Here both people keep restating their own positions. Nobody listens to anyone. The conversation sounds like this:
Blah, blah,
Yak, yak.
What I said was blah, blah.
Didn't you hear me say yak, yak? And so on....

1. Kitchen Sinking
This is what people do when they start out discussing one issue but then drift onto other topics. They often end up dragging "everything but the kitchen sink" into the conversation. Pretty soon both people get the feeling that they have to deal with all of the issues at once.

2. Yes But
Every time one person makes a suggestion, the other person finds something wrong with it. Partners sometimes are not aware of this habit.

3. Cross Complaining
Person A makes a complaint or request of Person B. Person B doesn't respond to that issue; instead, B brings up a complaint about person A….

4. Mind reading
Here one person assumes they know what the other person is "really" "Thinking or wanting."

5. Interrupting
Interrupting shows a lack of respect for what the other has to say.

6. Insulting Your Partner
Shows a lack of respect and love for the other person.

7. Threatening Your Partner
Instills fears and hate rather than create intimacy and love.

8. Airing Old Resentments
The tactic here is to avoid discussion of the issue at hand by always coming back to what your partner did wrong in the past.

9. Being Vague
Creates confusion, causes unclear communication and misunderstanding. For example, "you're driving funny today" is not specific.

10. Over generalizing - These statements usually begin with "you never" or "you always".

When Asking For a Behavioral Change
Describe
- Describe the other person's behavior objectively.
- Use concrete terms.
- Describe a specified time, place, and frequency of action.
- Describe the action, not the "motive."

Express
- Express your feelings.
- Express your feelings calmly.
- State feelings in a positive manner related to goal.
- Direct yourself to the specific offensive behavior, not the person.

Empathize
- Show some understanding of the other persons' position.
- Be honest, not sarcastic

Specify
- Ask explicitly for a change in behavior.
- Request a small change.
- Request only one or two changes at one time.
- Specify the actions you want to see stopped, and those you want to see performed.
- Take account of whether your person can meet your request without suffering huge loss.
- Specify what behavior you are willing to change to get the agreed change in behavior.

Consequences
- Make the consequences explicit.
- Give a positive reward for change in the desired direction.
- Select something that is desirable and reinforcing for the other person.
- Select a reward that is big enough to maintain the behavioral change.
- Select a punishment of magnitude that "fits the crime" of refusing to change behavior.
- Select a punishment that you are willing to carry out.

What change do you fear in your life at this time? Does the change involve your career, finances, relationships, business associations or affiliations?

The Benefits of Change

Change is often feared, however, nothing happens without change. Even though change is good for us, often it can cause us to feel tense and stressed. Think of change as a way to refine your goals in life or look at life from a different perspective. You may be stressed and not know it. Here are some symptoms of stress.

Symptoms of Stress

Symptoms of stress can be categorized as physical symptoms, behavioral symptoms, or emotional symptoms. After looking over the symptoms below, think about this past month. How many times have you experienced each of these symptoms? Example, one time, two times etc. Physical symptoms of a headache, stomachache, backache, muscle tension, diarrhea, heartburn, constipation, grinding teeth, skin rash, or a frequent need to urinate.

Beside your physical symptoms, you may experience other behavioral symptoms like blaming others, telling untruths, bossiness, irritability, impatience, anger, inflexibility, drinking, taking aspirin or pain relievers, have difficulty keeping commitments. Emotional symptoms include nervousness, anxiety, worry, fatigue, depression, fearfulness, and hopelessness, difficulty concentrating, forgetting important things, crying easily, or not being able to turn off certain thoughts.

Managing Stress, Stress and Cortisol

Your body's chemistry is altered by how you interpret events. Negative interpretations elevate your cortisol level, which suppresses our immune system, increases cholesterol, disturbs digestion, and causes insomnia. Exercise is the most beneficial tool to eliminate our stress response and to provide us a state of wholeness, and wellness. Exercise is the key, and its duration is vital. You must sustain your exercise period for a minimum of 20 minutes. Learn to modulate your intensity or pace until you can last for a prescribed duration. The prescribed level is frequently derived from the following equation: $80\% (220 - \text{your age}) = $ maximum target heartbeat. Exercise a minimum of 3 times per week to derive the benefits. Pick a Monday, Wednesday, Friday, or make it a family affair on Saturday. It is what works best for you.

Another stress elimination technique is the <u>Relaxation Response</u>. This is a conscious discipline, when practiced regularly alleviates the symptoms of stress. The directions are uncomplicated and with minimal effort can be accomplished be nearly everyone. Select a quiet uninterrupted place. Assume a comfortable sitting position, close your eyes, and let your body go limp by relaxing all of your muscles. Push all the busy thoughts out, and quiet your mind. Pay attention to your breathing and as you exhale, repeat to yourself the number ONE. The bottom line is, we can win against stress by being aware and taking the necessary action. An awareness of stress hormones and their accumulation is essential. The action steps are for us to work at decreasing our production of stress hormones and be proactive in its elimination.

There is a difference between complacency and satisfaction. If you are complacent, you are lying down on the job, but if you give satisfaction to God, yourself and others, you will enjoy a greater fullness of life. And fulfillment brings satisfaction.

Say to Yourself: I express God today, and I am filled with the joy of living. Every task I perform carries with it its own measure of satisfaction. I am always doing something that needs to be done, and when I fill this need, whether it is mine or someone else, I am creating satisfaction. Satisfaction is the state of my consciousness today. My every thought focuses on abundant supply. Therefore my every need is filled, and my every desire is gratified. There is order in the arrangement of my affairs, now and always. I think on divine order, and divine order is manifested in all areas of my life and affairs.

Affirm

I give thanks that the kingdom of Heaven is within me, and that I have come to know, God's eternal presence. Any incompleteness or shortcomings of my past are forgotten. There is only my consciousness of what I am and have today. My peace is the foundation of the inner work I have accomplished, and the trials I have surmounted. It is the handiwork of God working through me that gives me complete satisfaction. As I make this divine connection each day I dwell in the inner house of God."

LETTING GO

LETTING GO does not mean to stop caring-it means not to take responsibility for someone else.
LETTING GO is no to enable others-it's to allow learning from natural consequences.

LETTING GO is to admit your own powerlessness, which means the outcome is not in your hands.
LETTING GO is not to try to change or blame others-but to make the most of yourself.

LETTING GO is not to care for-but to care about.
LETTING GO is not to fix-but to be supportive.

LETTING GO is not to be in the middle arranging-but to be on the sidelines, cheering.
LETTING GO is not to be protective-it's to permit another to face reality.

LETTING GO is not to deny-but to accept.
LETTING GO is not to nag, scold or argue-it is to search out my own shortcomings and correct them.

LETTING GO is not to adjust everything to your desires-but to take each day as it comes, and cherish yourself in it.
LETTING GO is not to criticize and regulate others-but to grow and live for the future.
LETTING GO is to fear less, and love more. Anon

"Cast Your Burden On The Lord, And He Will Sustain You." (Psalm 55:22)

I AM WORTH IT

I may sometime cause confusion when I am unclear in my communication, unsure of myself, or uncertain about an outcome, yet I am worth the bother.
I may act timid and fearful sometimes, but please remember that I am trying to sort things out in my mind, and I am worth the bother.
Even though you may struggle to understand me, I am worth it.
My friend, I am the other half of you.
I am incomplete without you, and you are incomplete without me.
In some strange way, though we differ in racial composition, thoughts, ideas and behavior; we are wedded to each other.
I will release you for now, to soar above the heavens. Just remember that whatever disappointment or challenge I face, I deserve the best, for I am worth it.
      Ida Greene

SAY YES, I CAN

You've all that the greatest of men have had;
Two arms, two hands, two legs, two eyes,
And a brain to us if you would be wise,
With this equipment they all began.
So start from the top and say, "I can."

Look them over, the wise and the great,
They take their food from a common plate,
And similar knives and forks they use,
With similar laces they tie their shoes,
The world considers them brave and smart,

But you've all they had when they made their start.
You can triumph and come to skill,
You can be great if you only will.

You're well equipped for what fight you choose,
You have arms and legs and a brain to use,
An the person who has risen great deeds to do
Began their life with no more that you.
You are the handicap you must face,

You are the one who must choose your place.
You must say where you want to go,

How much you will study the truth to know;
God has equipped you for life, but He
Let's you decide what you want to be.
Courage must come from the soul within

The person must furnish the will to win.
So figure it out for yourself, my friend,
You were born with all that the great have had,
With your equipment they all began,
So, Get hold of yourself and say: "I CAN."
Anon

The New Black Family, African American Culture

It seems the American dream entails that we strive to better our life conditions, ourselves and our family life. To this we need to capitalize on the success models in place when I was young the motto was to do something to make your race proud. I would like to add to that and say we need to do something to make God proud of us. We are the children of God; since God does not make junk, our lives should be living testimonies of his goodness and greatness, and everything we do or say should be a success. Since the largest growing population in the United States today is the 85 years and older group, you will journey many times in your lifetime from success to success before you make your transition from planet earth. Often success is the result of patient persistence through failure. So do not become discouraged if you do not see instant results. We are all a diamond in the rough, trying to become our Divine Self through our many trials and tribulations. Jesus stated "Be of good cheer, for I have conquered the world." You must never quit striving to improve yourself or your life circumstances. Even though you may have challenges and it seems to takes a long time to reach your goals, it is worth it. Remember it is the journey of life not the destination that brings us joy.

Your success is created from your self expression. And your self-expression is a spiritual quality. You are here in life to express your God potential. Do not confuse your Divine self expression with your livelihood. When you allow God to express through you, all your needs will be met. Never accept a job, or engage in any activity just for money. Because if you do not express your Divine, God given talents, you will become disgruntled, bored, and lose enthusiasm for life and living. And when you lose your enthusiasm, you lose your light. Jesus said, "Ye are the light of the world." You are alive, joyous, and aglow when you do work you enjoy and it fulfills a divine purpose in the universe. You are a spiritual being, in a human body, having a spiritual experience. Your primary purpose to be on the planet is to use your divine self expression to grow spiritually, and become a Master like Jesus in your service to humanity. We must first master our physical body, before we achieve mastery in our spiritual life. And we do this through right thinking, right eating, right living, and right divine self expression.

To get answered prayers, remember to have an attitude of positive expectation and gratitude. Believe that God has heard you and will respond to your request. The mind of Christ Jesus is a mind of gratitude; it is a belief of knowing that God has answered you before your request is manifested. You are the light of the world let your light so shine before men that they will see your good works and glorify God. You are the light of the world therefore, if you are the light there will be no darkness. You are the salt of the earth and therefore you add the favor to life and living. God has called us to love and forgive each others; however, we must love ourselves first.

I am a Life Coach, I Coach people on Self development, developing Success Skills and Strategies that double your income, Leadership, Powerful Self -Expression and Empowerment, Business Management skills, Professional Speaking and Presentation Skills. For a 30 minute coaching or prayer session. I can be reached at (619) 262-9951. We are seeking people who want to be an Earth Angel by dong acts of kindness and love. If you are interested send us an e-mail to www.earthangel.org

Index

AIDS 96

Assertiveness Inventory 111

Business Ownership 80

Communication Skills 114

Domestic Violence 104

Down Lows 93

How to Avoid Money Anxiety and Worries 66

In Search of the Black Family 37

Prayer Treatment for Right Employment 72

Problem Solving 28

Sex Revolution 91

Signs of Low Self-Esteem 22

Symptoms of Stress 118

Tavis Smiley 25

The Black Church 99

Bibliography

1. *Light the Fire Within You*, Ida Greene, Ph.D., P.S.I. Publishers, 3639 Midway Drive, Suite B #374, San Diego, CA 92105

2. *Say Goodbye to Your Smallness, Say Hello to Your Greatness*, Ida Greene, Ph.D., P.S.I. Publishers, 3639 Midway Drive, Suite B #374, San Diego, CA 92105

3. *Anger Management Skills for Women and Men*, Ida Greene, Ph.D., P.S.I. Publishers, 3639 Midway Drive, Suite B #374, San Diego, CA 92105

Testimonials

Stirring Up the African American Spirit, addresses the complexities of today's society that challenges the black community.
      Toya Hicks

This book is a wake up call to the Black community. I was glued to each page for the outcome.
      Elizabeth Jones

These are thought provoking insights to a complex topic.
      James Maull, NBC Universal Studio

Dr. "Angel", Ida Greene has served as a stimulus to African American Business Women of Vision, in stirring up our souls to say goodbye to our smallness and hello to our greatness for many years. She sets the example of re-examining our own resourcefulness to continually discover the untapped greatness within us that is waiting to be used. We thank you, Dr. Greene for the prolific example you never fail to set.
      Dee Sanford, Business Motivational Speaker,
      Business Consultant and Trainer.
      Host of the Christian Business Forum TV Show

Printed in the United States
78114LV00003B/190-270